ADVENTUROUS PUB WALKS

IN

THE CHILTERNS

Jean Patefield

COUNTRYSIDE BOOKS
3 Catherine Road
Newbury, Berkshire

To view our complete range of books,
please visit us at
www. countrysidebooks co.uk

ISBN 978 1 84674 188 3

Designed by Peter Davies, Nautilus Design

Produced through MRM Associates Ltd., Reading
Typeset by Jean Cussons Typesetting, Diss, Norfolk
Printed in Thailand

CONTENTS

AREA MAP SHOWING THE LOCATION OF THE WALKS

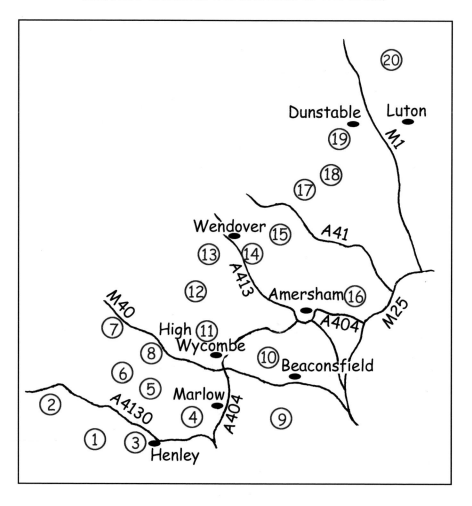

PUBLISHER'S NOTE

INTRODUCTION

The Chilterns are a range of chalk hills stretching in an arc about 40 miles north and west of London. This description is accurate but conveys nothing of the paradise they are for walkers. Within the 400 square miles encompassed by the Chilterns are about 1,500 miles of public footpaths, mostly very quiet, well signed and lovingly maintained.

The hills were formed about 26 million years ago as the result of a collision of truly epic proportions. The continental plate on which Africa rides crashed into the continental plate of Europe causing buckles and folds across Europe. The Alps are the most dramatic result but the same impact produced the Chilterns. To the north and west the scarp slope rises sharply and dramatically from the fertile Vale of Aylesbury and affords magnificent views (Walks 2, 13, 19 and 20). To the south and east the dip slope falls away gently to the River Thames. The western and eastern limits of the Chilterns are not so easy to define but are generally taken to be from Goring in the south-west to Ivinghoe Beacon (Walk 18) in the north-east. However, the Chilterns actually extend further north and east both in terms of landscape and the Area of Outstanding Natural Beauty, and this is explored by Walks 19 and 20.

Much of the charm of the Chiltern landscape comes from the valleys (Walks 5, 6 and 7), nearly all dry and locally called bottoms. These were formed in the Ice Age. The Chilterns were not covered by ice but were frozen much of the time. During the short sub-arctic summer, water flowed from the glaciers that lay a short distance north and eroded the valleys we see today.

The glory of the Chilterns is undoubtedly the beech woods for which they are famous: majestic without leaves in winter, carpeted with bluebells in spring (Walk 3), luminous green in summer and brilliantly aflame in autumn. The woods are not composed solely of beech, of course. Oak is common, along with many other species. Walk 9 explores the internationally important Burnham Beeches, which has a large number of magnificent ancient trees produced by pollarding.

It is the landscape of the Chilterns, designated as an Area of Outstanding Natural Beauty, which attracts the walker but throughout the region there are market towns and villages of great antiquity and interest. Many of the villages, such as Turville (Walk 8), Aldbury (Walk 17) and Hambleden (Walk 5), are gems of English vernacular architecture in perfect settings, while many of the market and coaching towns such as Wendover (Walk 14), Marlow (Walk 4) and Henley (Walk 3) have a great sense of place and are fascinating to explore.

The Ridgeway is a modern re-creation of an ancient trade route. It starts at Ivinghoe Beacon (Walk 18) and is used on several walks in this book, especially Walk 13.

The Chilterns are an ancient and managed landscape. The adventure of walking in the Chilterns does not come from exploring a wild and untamed area but from the variety and charm of the routes and the magnificent views, which I think surpass those of many more mountainous areas. The hills are not very high, about 800 feet at most, so there are no great peaks to be conquered and there are no local mountain rescue teams. However, do not underestimate the challenge these walks offer as a typical Chiltern outing is a switchback, up the hills, down into a valley then up the other side – usually several times!

All the routes are on public rights of way or permissive paths and have been carefully checked but, of course, in the countryside things do change; a gate replacing a stile is a common occurrence. In the Chilterns the footpaths are guarded by the Chiltern Society and nearly always marked by white or occasionally yellow or blue arrows. In areas where there is unrestricted public access such as Burnham Beeches (Walk 9), Ashridge (Walk 18) or Naphill Common (Walk 11) there are many other, unmarked paths and careful attention should be paid to the directions or you might have more of an adventure than you were anticipating!

Each walk is illustrated by a sketch map but it is also useful to carry the relevant Ordnance Survey map, especially to identify features in the views. The walks in this book are covered by sheets 171, 172, 181, 182, 192 and 193 in the Explorer series that are so good for walking.

There are many great pubs in the Chilterns, including the oldest free house in the country (Walk 10), which can perhaps trace its history back to Saxon times! Many, perhaps too many, have undergone a profound transformation in recent years. Nonetheless, there are lots of establishments from which to choose and I have tried to suggest those that retain a genuine pub ambience while serving good food in an attractive rural location. Some walks would better be described as 'adventurous pub crawls' as they pass so many pubs (notably Walks 1 and 10). Others pass only one, occasionally a few yards off the route.

The Chilterns is a superb area for walking with much of interest to enjoy on the way. I hope you get as much pleasure from exploring these routes as I did from preparing them – and enjoy the pubs as much as me.

Jean Patefield

STOKE ROW AND CHECKENDON
A woodland pub crawl

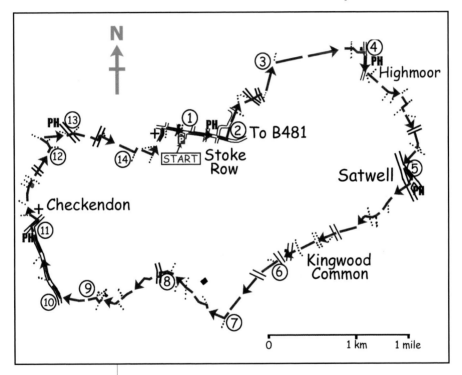

Distance:
8½ miles

Map: OS Explorer 171 Chiltern Hills West

Starting Point:
Stoke Row village hall. GR: 680840

How to get there: *From the B481, the Nettlebed–Reading road, at Highmoor, 1½ miles south of its junction with the A4130, take a minor road signed 'Stoke Row' for a mile to a car park behind the village hall on the left immediately after Stoke Row garage.*

THE MAHARAJAH'S WELL, SEEN AT POINT 14 OF THE WALK

*T*his excellent walk is really a woodland pub crawl, passing four hostelries well spaced out round the circuit, with a fifth just a few yards off the route. Despite the description, not all the way is through woodland – with fields, lanes and parkland making a pleasing contrast on this enjoyable walk. Most of the route *is* through the woods, however, and the discerning walker will notice that they are by no means all the same, the ecology of each wood reflecting differences in past management and underlying geology.

The **Dog and Duck** at Highmoor is a friendly, traditional Brakspear's house that serves a good selection of robust pub food, including filled baguettes and varieties of ploughman's at lunchtime. Open fires make this a cosy stopping place in winter and there is an extensive garden and covered patio for the warmer months. From here there is a view of a startling topiary – an oversized duck? – in the garden of a house across the road. Food is available every day except Monday.

Telephone: *01491 641261.*

Alternatives: The Four Horseshoes at Checkenden *(01491 680325)*, which is quite late on the route, welcomes walkers. The route also passes the Cherry Tree Inn near the start in Stoke Row *(01491 680430)* and the Lamb at Satwell *(01491 628482)*. A few yards off the route at point 13 is the Black Horse *(01491 680418)*.

 The Walk

❶ Turn right out of the car park through the village past the first of today's pubs, the **Cherry Tree**. When the footway ends continue ahead over the village green. *(0.3 mile)*

The village was once noted for its cherry trees, hence the name of the pub, and coach loads from Reading used to come to admire the blossom.

❷ At the far side of the village green turn left on a signed footpath that soon becomes a hedged path leading to a track. Turn left to a lane, then right along the lane. When the lane bends sharp left continue in the same direction along a signed bridleway. After 120 yards bear right, indicated by a waymark on a tree, to a lane in a dip. Cross the lane and carry on up the other side on a signed bridleway bearing right. Cross

another lane and press on along a surfaced drive. *(0.7 mile)*

❸ Some 40 yards after the entrance to **Little Farm** turn right over a stile next to a field gate. Bear slightly left across a field then on in the same direction from stile to stile, down into a dip and up the other side. At the top of the hill the path is enclosed on the right-hand side of a field and this then leads through a wood, into a small field and to the right of a house to emerge on a road. *(0.7 mile)*

❹ Turn right, past the **Dog and Duck**. Some 120 yards after the pub turn left into a wood on a signed path. Take the left option at a fork after 25 yards and ignore a path on the left after a further 30 yards. When the main path turns right by a field corner, bear slightly left on a rather fainter path, soon waymarked by yellow arrows on trees. Ignore a path on the right after 100 yards and continue ahead for a further

60 yards and now turn right to reach a T-junction after 200 yards. Turn right, following a waymarked path, for 80 yards and now turn left on a waymarked path to a stile out of the wood after 100 yards. Keep ahead across a field to a lane. Cross the lane and press on in the same direction back into the woods on a signed path. Towards the far end of the wood bear right at a fork to continue in the wood and emerge at a road junction. *(1 mile)*

5 Turn left, signed 'Shepherds Green', to the **Lamb**. Immediately before the pub turn right on a tiny lane, signed 'Peppard 2 Reading 8'. Cross a road and keep ahead on a signed bridleway starting along a track. Follow the path, initially at the edge of the wood then downhill, ignoring a path branching left, to reach a major fork. Bear right. Go over a cross path at the bottom of the hill and up the other side. At the top of the hill go over a tiny lane and keep ahead on a signed bridleway, forking right after 10 yards. Cross a lane and continue on the bridleway past **Holly Tree Cottage** to reach a more substantial lane. *(1.3 mile)*

6 Maintain direction, starting along a gravelled track but soon back in the woods. Ignore a path forking right by an unexpected streetlight. Cross a drive, now on a pleasant fenced and tree-lined path between fields as far as a stile on the right after a bare ½ mile *(0.6 mile)*

7 Turn right over the stile and walk along the left-hand side of a field to a signed path on the left. Turn left into woodland once more. Watch for a stile on the left. Cross this and turn right to continue in more or less the same direction with a wire fence on the right and ignoring paths to the left as far as a gate on the right. *(0.5 mile)*

8 Turn left downhill to a lane. Cross the lane to a signed footpath some 25 yards to the left and follow this uphill. Follow the path, waymarked with yellow arrows, as it climbs gently and ignore all side turns to reach a T-junction with a bridleway, marked by blue arrows on a post, near an attractive woodland cottage. Turn left for 10 yards then right to continue on the path to shortly reach a surfaced drive. *(0.6 mile)*

9 Turn left to eventually reach a lane. *(0.3 mile)*

10 Turn right to Checkendon and the **Four Horseshoes** on the left at a T-junction. *(0.5 mile)*

There has been a village here for a very long time. In the Domesday Book Checkendon is referred to as Cecadene, which means Ceca's pasture or settlement. The first

*church may have
been one of
several founded
by St Birinus, a
missionary sent in
AD 634 by Pope
Honorius I. The
present building
dates mainly from
the 12th century
but every era has
made its
contribution from
the 14th-century
wall paintings, the
15th-century
tower, Victorian
pews and 20th-century windows.
One of these commemorates the
life of Eric Kennington, a noted
war artist and sculptor, who was a
churchwarden here.*

THE DOG AND DUCK, HIGHMOOR

right, almost back on yourself, on a
waymarked path to a T-junction with
a track on a bend. Turn right to
continue in the same direction to a
lane. *(0.3 mile)*

⓫ Turn right. Immediately before
the church turn left on a signed path
starting along a drive lined with
clipped yew. Just before some gates
turn right through a gap in the fence
and follow the path to a stile on the
right. Go over the stile and bear left
across a small field to a stile by a
field gate. Follow the broad path
ahead, passing a pond on the right
and ignoring paths to left and right,
to a lane. Cross the lane and keep
ahead on a fenced path then on
across a field to a stile. *(0.7 mile)*

⓬ Over the stile turn left along a
track for 170 yards then turn sharp

⓭ Turn left for 10 yards (the **Black
Horse** is a few yards further along
the lane) where two paths are signed
'Stoke Row 1'. Take the one on the
right over a stile and walk along the
left-hand side of a field. When the
wood on the left ends, keep ahead to
a stile onto a lane. Turn left for 40
yards then right over a stile. Follow
the path by a hedge on the right
over a drive and ahead to a gate into
a belt of woodland to meet a cross
path. *(0.5 mile)*

⓮ Turn left and stay on the path as
it turns sharp right to a T-junction
with a track. Turn left. This leads into

Stoke Row. At the main road turn right, past the **Maharajah's Well**, back to the start. *(0.5 mile)*

Stoke Row, like many hilltop villages in the Chilterns, suffered grievously from a lack of water and this restricted its development. A local man, Mr Edward Anderdon Reade of Ipsden, became Governor of the North-west Provinces in India. He told the Maharajah of Benares about a boy from Stoke Row whom his mother beat because he drank the last of the water in the house during a drought. At that time it took a round trip of several miles to collect some more. The Maharajah was so touched by the story that he financed the digging of a well along with a keeper's cottage and a cherry orchard to provide for the upkeep of the well. Mr Reade designed the Indian-style cupola that stands over the 364-ft deep well. In 1863 when the well was opened for use, people flocked here to see this unusual structure with its golden dome. It eventually fell into disuse but was renovated in the 1950s.

The keeper's cottage is still beside it and the cherry orchard is now an ornamental garden.
Once the Maharajah's Well secured the water supplies, Stoke Row was able to grow. As well as being involved in agriculture, the inhabitants of this village, like so many others in the Chilterns, used to make chair parts from the local beech. Stoke Row was also noted for making wooden tent pegs, mainly because it was near the Royal Army Ordnance Depot at Didcot, and millions were made in both World Wars. Apparently, Government inspectors went sent around to pass or reject the pegs. Not knowing anything at all about tent peg making, but probably feeling it was up to them to make some sort of demonstration of knowledge, they would pass almost every pile and then choose one that they would demolish with a kick of their foot, marking a few of the pegs with a black arrow denoting rejection. The peggers would gather these up and shave off the offending mark ready for the next batch – which, needless to say, passed the test!

Date walk completed:

NUFFIELD
Views of the Vale

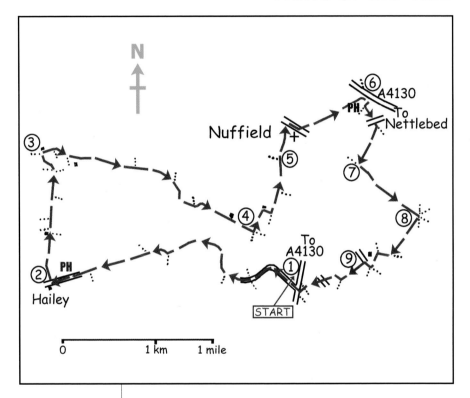

Distance:	Map: OS Explorer 171 Chiltern Hills West
8 miles	

Starting Point:
Ipsden Heath.
GR: 667856

How to get there: *From the A4130, the Henley–Wallingford road, about 1½ miles west of Nettlebed, take a minor road to Nuffield. Follow this for about 1½ miles, going through the village, to a tiny lane on the right, signed 'Homer Farm'. Turn along this to reach an informal layby on the right almost immediately. If this is full, there are other spots further along the lane where a car can be left without causing inconvenience.*

LOOKING OVER THE THAMES VALLEY AT POINT 5 OF THE WALK

*T*his walk explores the north-western edge of the Chilterns. The scarp slope is not as steep here as it is further east but nonetheless affords splendid views of the Oxfordshire Plain, the Vale of the White Horse and the Berkshire Downs. It is a route especially suited to winter because much of the way is on restricted byways, old tracks that never became surfaced roads but which offer good firm walking when other routes can be unpleasantly muddy. I think the views are better in winter too. The route also touches the village of Nuffield, whose wide common is used as a golf course, and the hamlet of Hailey, both with pubs.

The **Crown** at Nuffield, a Brakspear's house, is an attractive old pub that has been brought bang up to date in a sympathetic way and retains many of its original features. It has a pleasant enclosed garden at the rear as well as some outdoor tables at the front. For lunch there is a choice of sandwiches or light dishes such as, on my visit, crayfish and avocado salad, as well as full meals. One innovative idea is that the Crown serves coffee and pastries in the morning from 10 am.

The landlord at the Crown is happy for you to leave your car in his car park, a particularly good idea if you wish to stoke up on coffee and pastries before setting off (from point 6).

Telephone: *01491 641335.*

Alternatives: Quite early in the walk, the route also passes the King William at Hailey, a remote pub, full of character *(01491 681845)*. It offers excellent views from the many tables outside and sells walking sticks to help you on your way!

The Walk

❶ Continue along the lane, which becomes a track after about ½ mile, taking the left option when the track forks as it emerges from a wood and the views open up. Just before the **King William** the track becomes a lane again. *(2 miles)*

❷ Some 150 yards after the pub, opposite **Paddock End**, turn right on a signed path along a track. Keep ahead at some farm buildings in a dip and ignore tracks to left and right. When the track takes a sharp right-hand turn, maintain direction on a signed path across a field then on through a wood to a T-junction

with a track in front of a farm. *(0.9 mile)*

❸ Turn right and follow the track, forking left in front of a farm building to soon climb to the entrance to a wood. Press on through the wood ignoring all side turns. *(1.6 mile)*

From here, as from other spots in this part of the walk, there are excellent views across the Oxfordshire Plain. The hills crowned with trees are properly the Sinodun Hills but are universally known as Wittenham Clumps.

❹ About 300 yards after passing a farmhouse, turn left on a waymarked path leading towards some buildings along the left-hand side of a field. Follow the path round to the right in front of a fence to a stile onto a drive. Cross the drive and continue on the path to soon emerge in fields at the end of a hedge. Carry on along the path to the left of the hedge, passing a path on the right, to a T-junction with the **Ridgeway** (see Walk 13) on a bend. *(0.6 mile)*

5 Turn right along the Ridgeway, signed 'Nuffield 0.4 miles', to carry on in the same direction to a lane. Turn right along the lane past the church. At the far end of the church, turn left on a signed path to continue along the **Ridgeway**. This leads across a golf course (waymark posts show the line of the path) to reach the end of a track that shortly leads to a main road and the **Crown** while the **Ridgeway** continues to the left across the main road. *(0.8 mile)*

The name of this modest Oxfordshire village is known throughout the world due to the life and works of William Morris, Lord Nuffield. He left school at fifteen, and worked in Oxford, first as a repairer and maker of bicycles, then a maker of motor cycles and finally of cars. He was one of the first British industrialists to introduce mass production methods. From the first Morris Oxford of 1913 to the still familiar post-war Morris Minor, his Morris and MG cars were known around the world. Lord Nuffield was made a viscount in 1938, and took the name of this village where he had settled near his favourite golf course. He is famous not only as an industrialist but also as a man who gave away as much money as he made – at least £30 million in his lifetime, worth far more today. Personally frugal, he gave money to hospitals and medicine (the Nuffield hospitals), to education (Nuffield College, Oxford), to depressed areas and to the armed forces. He died in 1963 and lies under a modest slab by Holy Trinity church.

6 Immediately after the pub turn right along a track and after a few yards bear half left on a waymarked path back across the golf course to a road. Cross the road and continue on the path across a fairway for 60 yards to two waymark posts about 15 yards apart, marking a fork in the path. Follow the path waymarked by the right-hand post to reach a stile off the golf course. Carry on across a field to a stile onto a cross path. *(0.5 mile)*

This golf course has been here since 1901 and is considered to be one of the finest inland courses in the country.

7 Over the stile, turn left and follow the path to a T-junction with a track. *(0.5 mile)*

THE CROWN PUB, NUFFIELD

8 Turn right for 15 yards to a stile on the right into a field. Head across the field on, at the time of writing, quite a faint path, taking a line to the right of a clump of trees, then heading to the left of a farm seen ahead. Go over a stile by a field gate at the far side of the field and follow the clear track to the right to a T-junction. Turn left and follow this around farm buildings, ignoring turns to the left, to the start of a surfaced lane. *(0.5 mile)*

9 Turn left on a signed, hedged path. When the enclosing hedges end, press on along the right-hand side of a field with extensive views across **Reading**. Go over a cattle grid onto a surfaced drive and follow this

for 80 yards then turn right, passing to the right of a tennis court, to a stile. Over the stile bear half left to a stile onto a tiny lane. Cross the lane to another stile. Now bear half right across a field to yet another stile, this time into a wood. Follow the path through the wood, carpeted with bluebells in season (see Walk 3), across a farm track to a road opposite the lane to **Homer Farm** where this walk started. *(0.5 mile)*

Date walk completed:

19

HENLEY AND ROTHERFIELD GREYS
The bluebell walk

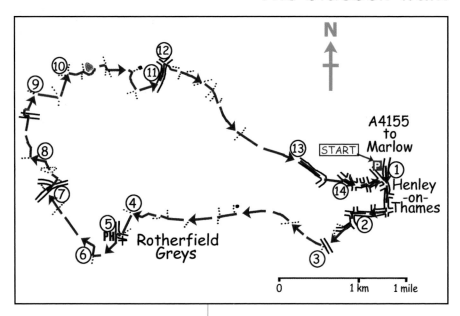

Distance:
8½ miles

Map: OS Explorer 171 Chiltern Hills West

Starting Point:
Dry Leas car park, Henley (charge). GR: 760831. If this car park is full, there are other signed long stay car parks in Henley from which you can make your way to the traffic lights in the centre of town at the junction of Bell Street, Market Place, Hart Street and Duke Street to pick up the route partway through point 1 at *.

How to get there: Dry Leas car park is at the edge of Henley on the A4155 to Marlow, 100 yards from its junction with the A4130. It is next to Henley Rugby Club.

THE WOODS ARE A MASS OF BLUEBELLS IN THE SPRING

*T*his exceptionally attractive walk to the west of Henley is worth doing at any time of year but we always try and fit it in during early May because the display of bluebells in the second half is so breathtaking. The blue of the flowers mirroring the sky above and the air filled with their scent is an experience to be treasured. The route starts and finishes in Henley-on-Thames, which is said to be the oldest town in Oxfordshire and is well worth exploring.

The **Maltsters Arms** in Rotherfield Greys, originally called the Shovel and Broom, was opened in the late 18th century by Robert Appleton, a rival brewer to Robert Brakspear in Henley. In 1803 Joseph Benwell came in and took the pub off their hands. Later, in 1812, the two companies, Benwell and Brakspear, amalgamated and the Maltsters Arms has been a Brakspear's house to this day. The cosy bars reflect this long history and have a wealth of cricketing memorabilia, including some original cartoons. Outside there is an enclosed and sheltered patio leading to a pleasant beer garden. The lunchtime menu features old favourites, for example, ham, egg and chips or pie and mash, as well as daily specials or lighter meals such as a delicious eggs Benedict and filled paninis.

Telephone: *01491 628400.*

Alternatives: There are, of course, numerous pubs as well as other eating establishments of all kinds in Henley but nowhere else on the route.

 *The Walk*

❶ Return to the road and turn right. At a roundabout bear slightly left to walk along **Bell Street** into the middle of **Henley**. * At the traffic lights turn right along **Market Place**, going to the left of the town hall, signed 'Peppard', and follow this road for about 300 yards. *(0.6 mile)*

Henley is a very attractive town and interesting to explore with over 300 listed buildings of many styles and periods. Its position on the Thames and the road to London has always been important and it became established in the 12th century as a river crossing and port for the supply of timber and grain along the river to the capital. In the 18th century Henley was a coaching stop between London and Oxford and there was much rebuilding and refronting of houses at this period. There are many coaching inns including the Red Lion, which boasted Charles I, Boswell and George III among its visitors.

❷ Turn left on **Paradise Road** and take the first right, still Paradise Road and signed 'The Henley College Rotherfield Buildings'. As the road bears right to the college after 175 yards keep ahead on a path signed 'Greys Green 2½'. Maintain the same direction as the path joins a surfaced path to reach a road. *(0.3 mile)*

❸ Cross the road and carry on in the same direction along the bottom of a valley, crossing a path**, and continue through a small copse and ahead as you join a track from the right. When the track bears left and uphill, leave it, right, to carry on along the valley path. At the end of the field go over a stile on the right and press on along the left-hand side of two further fields and into a third field for 230 yards. *(1.6 mile)*

** *Today this is a peaceful and prosperous area but there was much poverty before improved communications attracted wealthy commuters and, apparently, highway robbery used to be rife. This path is called Pack and Prime Lane. The name is said to come from the days when the London to Oxford coach would stop to 'pack and prime' the guns they carried as protection.*

4 Turn left over a stile into a wood and climb out of the valley through the wood. At the top of the slope continue across a field towards the church to a road and the **Maltsters Arms** to the right. *(0.2 mile)*

Rotherfield Greys is an ancient community, mentioned in the Domesday Book under the ownership of the Norman knight Anchetil de Greye. Rotherfield comes from the Anglo-Saxon 'redrefeld', meaning cattle lands. The church is basically Norman but was much 'improved' by the Victorians. It contains the 16th-century Knollys Chapel, which houses the ornate tomb of Robert Knollys, Elizabeth I's treasurer who

took charge of Mary Queen of Scots during her imprisonment; and of Robert's wife Katherine, a first cousin to Elizabeth I; and the effigies of their 16 children. The Knollys family owned nearby Greys Court, now in the care of the National Trust, which is not visited on this route but the lovely gardens are worth seeing. The church curate reported in 1738 that his parishioners were so poor that of the 'Absenters from ye Church there are a great many yet come but seldom [for] want of clothes' – or at least that is what he thought! In 1823 Revd J. Ingram wrote of his efforts to create jobs by cultivating opium: 'From its purity it was found of superior efficacy to that bought from Turkey or the East Indies, and I obtained a high price for it from the Society of Apothecaries Hall.'

5 Take a signed path between the pub and the church and this soon leads across fields to a gate onto a hedged track. *(0.3 mile)*

6 Turn right to eventually reach a road. *(0.6 mile)*

7 Turn right along the road as far as a junction. Turn left then immediately right on a clear but unsigned path that leads to a T-junction with a track in front of a high wooden fence. Turn left and this soon becomes a path that leads into a wood. Some 10 yards into the wood fork right, ignoring a path along the right-hand side of the wood. At the far end of the wood go over a stile on the right and follow the path to a second stile onto a surfaced track. *(0.4 mile)*

8 Turn left for about 100 yards then turn right on a signed path that leads down into a valley and up the other side to a lane. Turn left for 40 yards then turn right on a signed path next to a concrete drive and follow this down into the next valley. *(0.6 mile)*

These woods are particularly beautiful in late April and early May when the woodland floor is carpeted with bluebells. In recent years there has been much concern about the genetic purity of our native bluebell. A closely related strain known as the Spanish bluebell, originating from Western Spain and Portugal, was first introduced as a garden plant around 1680 and has, of course, escaped and hybridised with the English variety. The original English bluebell is quite delicate with the deep blue flower bells just on one side of the stalk, which tends to bend over. Spanish bluebells are more robust with an upright flower-stalk and paler flower bells, often with even paler stripes, all round the stem. The native species has a strong scent whereas the interloper is almost scentless. Whether this is a dreadful threat to one of our best-loved and iconic native flowers or part of the evolution of this species, albeit brought about by human actions, depends on your point of view.

9 Turn right along the valley bottom. At the end of the valley ignore an uphill path on the left and go ahead a few yards to a second, more level, path on the left. Follow this for about ¼ mile. *(0.4 mile)*

10 Turn right on a waymarked path to climb out of the valley, ignoring paths on the right and left. At the top pass a pretty reservoir and go over a stile. Turn left to a second stile. Over this, turn right to walk along the right-hand side of a field to a stile onto a cross track. Turn right for 40 yards then go over a stile on the left into a wood. After a few yards turn left on a waymarked path. Ignore a path on the left leading, at the time of writing, to a pink-washed house and continue inside the wood to reach a cross path, which is not all that obvious, about 50 yards after a field on the left ends. Turn left to stay just inside the wood to a lane. *(1 mile)*

11 Turn left. *(0.2 mile)*

12 At a road junction at the entrance to **Greenmarsh Farm**, turn right along a track for 35 yards then bear right on an initially less than obvious path. (If you reach the point where the track is surfaced you have gone about 15 yards too far.) This path leads almost back to **Henley**. At first it is rather faint and is

THE MALTSTERS ARMS, ROTHERFIELD

almost parallel to the track but it soon diverges and becomes a bit more obvious. It is waymarked by arrows on trees. You need to watch for these to stay on the correct route as this is open access woodland and there are many informal paths. In particular, some 200 yards after leaving the track ignore an unmarked path on the right and then, when the path forks after a further 50 yards, bear right as directed by a yellow arrow nailed to a tree. Subsequent waymarks are painted on the trees. Keep ahead at a waymarked cross path, the correct path now numbered 25, and ignore all further paths to right and left, some waymarked and some not, to eventually reach a golf course. Follow the path in the same direction across the golf course, following a line of trees. This gradually becomes a better defined track. *(1.3 mile)*

⓭ When the track ends, take the stile ahead onto a drive that soon becomes a minor road. After ¼ mile it makes a sharp bend right and there is a public footpath on the left. Take this downhill into **Henley**. *(0.4 mile)*

⓮ Turn right at the road, downhill. At the T-junction turn right and then first left into **Badgemore Lane**. At the main road turn right and at the roundabout turn left on **Marlow Road**, which leads back to the car park. *(0.5 mile)*

Date walk completed:

MARLOW AND MEDMENHAM
Beside the Thames

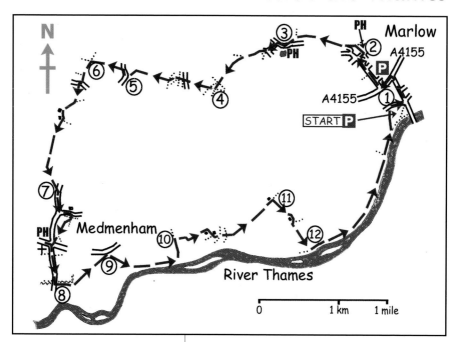

Distance:
9½ miles

Starting Point:
Pound Lane car park, Marlow
(charge). GR:848862.
Alternatively, park in Central
car park (charge) on Riley Road
behind Waitrose. Turn right out
of the car park to Oxford Road
to pick up the route partway
through point 1.

Map: OS Explorer 172 Chiltern Hills East

How to get there: *Directions are given from
the car park in Pound Lane, Marlow. This is
just off the High Street, a couple of hundred
yards on the town side of Marlow Bridge.*

MARLOW BRIDGE

*T*he southern edge of the Chilterns is the mighty River Thames. This route explores the high ground behind Marlow where there are some outstanding stretches through the woods that crown the hills. The walk continues to the ancient riverside village of Medmenham, which has a long, though not always glorious, history. The return leg is essentially beside the river though on the northern, Chiltern, side the path is forced away from the river at times.

The **Dog and Badger** at Medmenham is said to date from the 14th century so it was already old when Nell Gwynne stayed here. It wears its years lightly, however, and is now an attractive combination of ancient

27

and modern with open fires in the winter and a pleasant garden and patio for the warmer months. Don't forget to inspect the Civil War cannonball dug out of a wall. For a light lunch there is a tempting selection of sandwiches served with salad and crisps or a choice of omelettes or salads. Bigger appetites will find plenty to satisfy them on the full restaurant menu. The real ales are Fuller's London Pride and Rebellion IPA.

Telephone: *01491 571362.*

Alternatives: As well as the numerous pubs in Marlow, the route passes the Royal Oak *(01628 488611)* in Bovingdon Green early in the walk. Teas are served at Temple Lock overlooking the Thames.

 *The Walk*

1 From the car park, turn right along **Pound Lane** then left up the **High Street** to the far end. Turn left along **West Street** then right along **Oxford Road**. Take the fourth road on the right, **Queens Road**, for 50 yards. *(0.7 mile)*

Marlow is an ancient and prosperous town with many Georgian buildings hidden behind modern shop fronts and it is well worth taking the time to explore. The imposing building looking down the High Street, now a shop, was originally the Town Hall, built in 1807. The obelisk outside was erected by the Reading and Hatfield Turnpike Trust, led by the Cecil family of Hatfield House. The Marquess of Salisbury of Hatfield House was a

martyr to gout. Every year in the social season he travelled to Bath or Cheltenham in order to take the waters and one purpose of the road improvement was to shorten the bumpy, agonizing journey from Hatfield to the Bath road at Reading. It thus became known as the Gout Track. West Street, along which we walk, has attracted several poets. Shelley lived at number 104. After his first wife drowned herself he married his mistress Mary and it was while living in Marlow that she wrote Frankenstein. *Shelley was introduced to Marlow by another poet, Thomas Love Peacock, who also lived in West Street, at number 47. In more modern times T.S. Eliot moved to Marlow with his wife and they lived at number 31 West Street. He travelled to London every day by cycling to Maidenhead to catch the train.*

2 Immediately before the **Duke of Cambridge** turn left on a signed path and follow this up past some allotments on the right to a drive. Turn left for 20 yards then right, now joining the **Chiltern Way**, to emerge on a road opposite the **Royal Oak**. *(0.6 mile)*

3 Turn right past the pub and village pond. Take the first lane on the left, still on the **Chiltern Way**, signed 'Bovingdon Green'. At a T-junction turn right. When the surfaced lane shortly ends, follow a track round to the left. When the track ends, continue along a fenced path, ignoring a path to the left, and press on ahead as the path enters a wood to reach a cross path in a slight dip. There are two rising paths ahead: take the one on the left, following the **Chiltern Way** waymark, to reach a cross path after 100 yards. *(0.7 mile)*

4 Turn right and follow the path, aided by occasional white arrows on trees, to a lane. Cross the lane and carry on along the path, passing an information board about the use of these woods in the First World War for training, to a complex junction after 75 yards. Take the waymarked path half right downhill into a valley and up the other side to a stile into a field. Immediately over the stile, turn left and walk along the left-hand side of two small fields to a lane. *(0.8 mile)*

5 Turn right for 50 yards then turn left on a track through **Homefield Wood** for about ¼ mile. *(0.3 mile)*

6 Turn left on a waymarked cross path, leaving the **Chiltern Way**, up through conifers out of the valley. Carry on in the same direction when the path joins a track to a lane. Cross the lane to a path 20 yards to the right and walk the length of a field to a gate. Keep ahead across a small field and past farm buildings to walk along a farm drive. Just after a pair of cottages on the right, bear right on a signed path. Keep roughly equidistant between a wood on the right and a hedge on the left to a stile. Over the stile, bear left to a stile by a gate onto a lane. *(1.2 mile)*

7 Turn right as far as the first lane on the left. Turn sharp left along **School Lane**, to the left of the entrance to **States House**, for 200 yards. Take a signed path on the right opposite a house, shortly crossing a drive. Some 30 yards after the drive turn right on the waymarked path* and follow this back to the lane, bearing right when the path forks just after an information board. Turn left to a main road and the **Dog and**

Badger lies a few yards to the right. To continue the route, cross the main road and walk along **Ferry Lane** through **Medmenham**. *(1 mile)*

People have lived here by the Thames from time immemorial. This path* crosses the remains of the prehistoric hillfort known as Medmenham Camp, built in a

commanding position at the end of a spur overlooking the Thames Valley. The site was probably occupied for many thousands of years. It is likely that the fortifications date back to at least the Iron Age, more than 2,000 years ago, but may well be older than that as numerous worked flints have been found in the area.

THE DOG & BADGER IN MEDMENHAM

The church is supposed to have been founded in AD 640 by Birinus (see Walk 1); the present structure dates from the 12th century and was heavily restored in 1839. A Cistercian monastery was founded here in the 12th century but never prospered and by the time of the Dissolution there was only one monk besides the abbot. Its fame comes from its association with the Hell Fire Club. In 1755 it was acquired by Sir Francis Dashwood of West Wycombe. He used it as a venue for the Brotherhood of St Francis or Dashwood's Apostles, often called the Hell Fire Club, which included many of the most prominent men in the country among its members. This was the ideal, discreet site since it could be approached from the river and was screened by trees: paparazzi were a problem in those days too. Workmen were sent in, the abbey site was rebuilt and the grounds landscaped to make it suitable for the wild parties held there. It is said to have housed the largest collection of pornography in England at the time. There were accusations of Satanism, especially after Dashwood and the Earl of Sandwich attended a church service at St Peter's where Sandwich apparently let loose a small baboon into the church. The regular devotees

fled in horror, convinced that the Devil himself had invaded their place of worship. However, orgies rather than Devil worship are more likely and the latter was probably a political slur.

8 Immediately after a small bridge over a stream, turn left on a track to the left of **Monks Cottage**. This soon becomes a path by a stream then bears left across small fields to a drive. Turn left back to the main road. *(0.5 mile)*

9 Turn right and immediately bear right along a signed path on a surfaced drive to the **Thames**. Follow the fenced path beside the river, then climbing above the river, looking down on **Hurley Lock**, and through a tunnel. *(0.8 mile)*

The cliffs to your left are in the extensive grounds of Danesfield House. It has been suggested that the name indicates that the site was a Danish encampment, hence 'Danes-field'. Whether or not that is so, finds have shown it was inhabited long before that. The present house was built in 1900 and is now a hotel and spa. From the opposite bank of the Thames it looks very imposing, but the path here is kept well out of sight, partly by the tunnel you have just walked through.

10 When the wall on the right ends, turn sharp right. When the path becomes a gravelled drive, continue past **Home Farm House** to Harleyford Golf Club buildings. A few yards after the track is surfaced, it bends right. Go ahead on a surfaced path and follow the signed path between the buildings, across a drive and down through woodland into a timber yard and on across another drive. Bear round to the left to a kissing gate to the left of a field gate. Follow a path close to a fence on the left to a track by a house. *(0.9 mile)*

11 Turn right on a surfaced drive to a farm taking the path to the left past the house then returning to the drive. Continue on the surfaced drive to the river, ignoring a track on the left. *(0.5 mile)*

12 Turn left on a path along the river bank. Follow this back to **Marlow**. As you approach the town, take a surfaced path on the left through the park back to the start. *(1.3 mile)*

Temple Lock is about 100 yards to the right as you reach the river. Teas are served in the garden of the lock keeper's cottage at weekends from Easter onwards and during the summer holidays. This is beautifully situated on an island overlooking a lovely stretch of the river with the traffic through the lock to watch: just the place to idle away an hour on a sunny afternoon if you fancy some of the alternative amber nectar. The opening hours are somewhat flexible, depending rather on the weather since there is no indoor accommodation, but if the flag is flying, they are serving. Telephone: 01628 824333.

Date walk completed:

THE HAMBLEDEN VALLEY
A Chiltern panorama

THE VILLAGE OF HAMBLEDEN

Distance:
8 miles

Map: OS Explorer 171 Chiltern Hills West

Starting Point:
Hambleden village car park next to the Stag and Huntsman pub. GR: 785865

How to get there: *At Mill End, 3 miles from Henley and 5 miles from Marlow on the A4155, the Henley–Marlow road, turn up the road signed 'Hambleden 1, Skirmett 3, Fingest 3'. Turn right into Hambleden village on a road signed 'Pheasant's Hill 1 Frieth 3 Lane End 4'. In the centre of the village, when the main road bends left, continue ahead on a lane past the Stag and Huntsman to a car park on the right.*

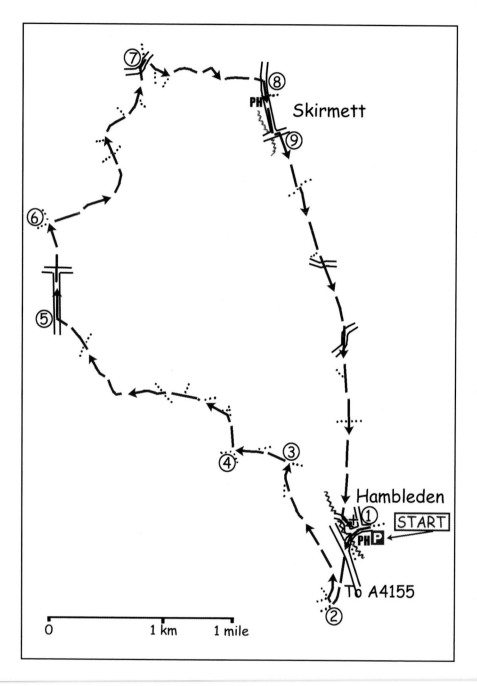

*T*his walk offers a panorama of the Chilterns in all their beauty and variety. Hambleden is a near perfect English village, with a historic manor house, a church that has been described as a miniature cathedral and, most importantly, a great pub. The first two-thirds of this route explores the woods on the west side of the valley and has some outstanding views. These are at their best in winter and spring before the leaves close them off, to at least some extent. In spring the woodland floor bears its crop of flowers to delight us – dog's mercury, violets, primroses and wood anemone. The trees give welcome shade on a hot summer's day and in the autumn they are breathtaking in their fiery hues. The route then drops back down into the valley to visit Skirmett and its welcome pub before an easy stroll along the valley bottom leads back to Hambleden.

The **Frog** in Skirmett is the pub for all seasons: it has a lovely garden with extensive views of the Hambleden Valley to enjoy in summer while in winter there is a roaring log fire with comfy seats in the public bar. Don't get too comfortable though – there are still a couple of miles to go! At lunchtime they serve a selection of baguettes with tasty fillings as well as the full menu, which changes with the seasons. They stock their own beer, Hopping Frog, brewed for them by Wadworth, as well as Rebellion IPA.

Telephone: *01491 638996.*

Alternatives: The Stag and Huntsman in Hambleden *(01491 571227)* next to the car park where this walk starts is an equally good choice, with a large and popular garden.

 *The Walk*

Hambleden is the quintessential English village, with its charming brick and flint cottages grouped round the pump and the chestnut tree in the village square and, as such, figures on every film location manager's list: you may have seen it, for example, in episodes of Midsomer Murders. In 1315 Hambleden was granted a charter *from Edward II to hold a fair. It was revived in 1864 and 1955 to raise money for the church and school. The fair took place on midsummer's eve and was discontinued a few years after its last revival because of rowdy behaviour. Many distinguished personages, including Queen Matilda and King John, have owned the manor and the village has several famous sons. Thomas de Cantilupe was Chancellor of England and Bishop of Hereford. He was the last pre-Reformation English saint and was born at the manor house in 1218. Adrian Scrope, who was one of the signatories to the death warrant of Charles I, came from Hambleden, as did Lord Cardigan, who led the Light Brigade into the 'Valley of Death'. A famous adopted son was W.H. Smith, the newsagent. He bought the Hambleden estate in 1870 and it was owned by the Smith family until 2007 when it was sold to a wealthy Swiss financier.*

1 Return to the lane and turn left. At the church bear left to the main road. Cross the road to a signed and surfaced path and follow the main path uphill, ignoring all small paths to the left. *(0.5 mile)*

2 Just as the path starts to descend, turn right on a signed bridleway to reach a cross path after about 70 yards. Turn right. Continue ahead as the path joins a track coming in on the left. *(0.8 mile)*

3 When the track bends sharp right, turn left uphill, remaining just inside the wood and emerging from the wood near the top of the hill. Turn left on a track to continue in much the same direction across a field and into another wood to meet a cross track some 50 yards into the wood. *(0.3 mile)*

4 Turn right. After 200 yards bear left off the track on a path signed by a yellow waymark on a post. Follow the waymarked path down into a valley, ignoring tracks that join. Cross a path along the bottom of the valley and press on up the other side to eventually reach the end of a concrete track. Turn left to a lane. *(1.3 mile)*

5 Turn right along the lane. At a T-junction continue ahead over a stile by a field gate to cross a field to another stile into a wood. Follow the path through the wood to meet a cross track in a dip. *(0.5 mile)*

6 Turn right along the track. As it approaches a gate into a field, bear slightly right to continue just inside the wood to eventually arrive at a lane. *(1.2 mile)*

7 Turn right along the lane for 150 yards and then turn right over a

THE GARDEN OF THE FROG PUB IN SKIRMETT

stile, back into the wood. Follow the path ahead through the wood, uphill straight across a field, ignoring a faint but signed path bearing right across the field, Go back into woodland to shortly meet a T-junction. Turn left and follow the path round the hill and down to the road in **Skirmett**. *(0.8 mile)*

From this path there are wonderful views across the upper Hambleden Valley, explored on Walk 8. The impressive white windmill on the hill across the valley was featured in the film **Chitty Chitty Bang Bang**. *This is one of the few left of the many that used to be found across the Chilterns. It is now a private house. After a wet winter you may be able to see the silver ribbon of Hamble Brook that sometimes flows down the valley below. It is a winterbourne – a stream that only flows when the water table in the underlying rock is high enough for water to come to the surface.*

8 Turn right through the village, passing the **Frog** on the right. When the main road bends right, turn left, signed 'Frieth 1¼ Lane End 2½', for 30 yards. *(0.3 mile)*

The name Skirmett is thought to

originate with Danish settlers from the words 'shire', an administrative area, and 'mot', a meeting place. It used to be a more complete community and had three pubs of which only the Frog, once called the King's Arms, now survives. The names of many of the houses tell of their former uses.

9 Turn right, signed 'The Chiltern Way'. The path leads along the bottom of the valley back to **Hambleden**. It is not very obvious to start with and lies near the left-hand side of the first field to a stile. After this stile it gets easier to follow from kissing gate to kissing gate, crossing a track and a lane. It joins another lane through the hamlet of **Colstrope** then takes to the fields again as the lane turns right. At this point be sure to stay well to the left to a small metal gate or you will end up on the wrong side of a hedge. Press on along the valley bottom and, as you get closer to Hambleden, the path leads along the bottom of some gardens. Soon after that **Hambleden church** with its distinctive tower and sheltering tree comes into view. As you

approach the church the path veers right across the field to a gate onto a lane. Turn left to the centre of the village and left again back to the start. *(2.3 miles)*

The church of St Mary was first built in Saxon times but the font is probably the only survivor from that date. The building we see today is Norman, though there has been much rebuilding and restoring down the ages. The Norman tower collapsed in 1703 and the present one was built eighteen years later. The monuments include one to Sir Cope D'Oyley, his wife and their ten children. The children shown holding skulls died before their parents. The inscription detailing the virtues of Lady D'Oyley is said to be by her brother, Francis Quarles, Poet Laureate, and is worth reading. Throughout the church, windows, brasses, plate and bells commemorate past rectors. The first known rector was appointed Archbishop of Canterbury in 1231 but the Pope vetoed his appointment because he was 'a mere secular courtier, hasty in speech and haughty in spirit'.

Date walk completed:

THE STONOR VALLEY
Flora and fauna

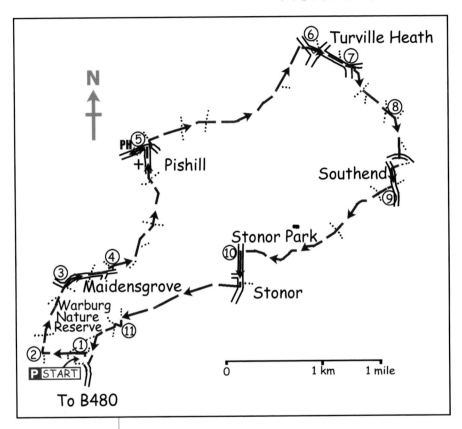

Distance:
7½ miles

Map: OS Explorer 171 Chiltern Hills West

Starting Point:
Warburg Nature
Reserve car park
(donation
suggested).
GR: 720878

How to get there: *Take the B480, which leads off the
A4130 about a mile north of Henley, through Lower and
Middle Assendon. At the north end of Middle Assendon
take a tiny lane signed 'Bix Bottom' and follow this for
about 2 miles until it ends at the reserve car park.*

39

STONOR HOUSE, SEEN FROM THE PATH

*T*his may be one of the shorter walks in this book but it punches well above its length in terms of variety and interest, and its several ascents totalling about 1,000 ft mean that it offers a reasonable challenge. It starts at Warburg Nature Reserve, the premier reserve of the Berks, Bucks and Oxon Wildlife Trust and lovely at all times of year whatever the weather. It climbs from there to explore the top of the Stonor Valley, a switchback route taking us through Pishill with its ancient church and pub before climbing to Turville Heath and Southend. The descent through Stonor Park is one of the finest paths in the Chilterns and truly memorable before a final climb over the ridge back to Warburg. There is a succession of outstanding views and this is Chiltern scenery of swooping dales and hills crowned with hanging woods at its very best.

The **Crown** at Pishill is everything a country pub should be and is deservedly popular despite its remote location. It was certainly a coaching inn during the 15th century and may well be able to trace its roots back to the 11th century. It has plenty of tables outside and a cosy interior with a log fire in winter. For a lighter lunch there is a choice of delicious sandwiches, ploughman's or that traditional favourite, rarely seen these days, pork pie served with a pickled egg and salad (we are in the health conscious 21st century after all!). There is a full menu of daily specials for those with a more robust appetite. The desserts are very tempting including, on my visit, coffee and frangelico brûlée or banana fritters with toffee sauce and ice cream. The Crown always has Brakspear's on tap accompanied by a guest beer, which is often, though not exclusively, from local breweries.

Telephone: *01491 638364.*

Alternatives: There is no other source of refreshment on this route.

 The Walk

❶ Go through a gate at the far end of the car park to a fork after 30 yards. Turn left and follow the grassy path through the reserve to reach a small gate into a wood and a sunken track after a further 25 yards. *(0.3 mile)*

This wonderful nature reserve is named after 'Heff' Warburg, the very distinguished botanist who died in 1966, a year before the site was acquired. Professor Warburg will always be remembered as one of the authors of the hugely authoritative **Flora,** *a descriptive list of all the plants of the British Isles, published in 1952 and always called 'Clapham, Tutin and Warburg' (or just 'CTW') after the three botanists who compiled*

it. The site is especially famous for its flora, with more than 450 species of plants recorded, including 15 wild orchids. Forty different kinds of butterfly have been spotted here too, as well as 450 moths and 950 fungi. It occupies the sides of a dry valley and is a noted frost pocket, making it even more lovely when everything is covered with hoar on a clear and cold morning.

❷ Turn right and follow the track up to a lane. *(0.4 mile)*

❸ Turn right along the lane. *(0.3 mile)*

❹ Immediately after a lane to **Maidensgrove village** on the right, turn left on a signed path starting along a track. When the track appears to end at gates, continue on the path to the left. Keep ahead as a path joins from the right after 40 yards and follow the waymarked path close to the left-hand side of the wood, ignoring a path to the right, then steeply downhill to a cross track. Do not turn left on the track but keep ahead for a couple of yards then bear slightly left on a waymarked bridleway along the right-hand side of a field. At the end of the field join a track coming in from the left and keep ahead when this becomes a tiny lane past **Pishill church** to a T-junction. *(1 mile)*

There are two accounts of how Pishill got its name. The first is that it comes from 'pisum', the Latin for 'pea', because of the many pea farms that were once in this area. The other, supported by the Crown pub, is that it used to be Pisshill because the wagonners and their horses would take a comfort break here as they climbed over the Chilterns.

❺ Turn left for 200 yards to the **Crown** then return to this point and

THE PUB AT PISHILL

continue along the road for 50 yards. As the road turns right, turn left on the **Oxfordshire Way** along a track for 30 yards then turn right over a stile on an initially fenced path. Press on across a roughly surfaced track then down into a dip and steeply up the other side, past a spot with a wonderful view and a seat from which to enjoy it. At the top the way becomes more of a fenced track. When this turns right maintain direction through a metal kissing gate and across three fields to a drive. Turn right to emerge on a lane at a junction. *(1.5 mile)*

6 Take the further of the two lanes on the right, signed 'Turville 2¼ Fingest 2¼'. Shortly keep ahead over a cross lane to the next junction. Keep ahead again, this time signed 'Turville 2 Fingest 2', for 20 yards. *(0.3 mile)*

7 Turn right next to a green utility box on what seems to be an unsigned path, to find the sign a few yards into the wood. Follow the path through the trees. Keep ahead at a cross path marked by waymark arrows on a post. Immediately after passing through a gap in a fence the path forks. This is not that obvious on the ground at the time of writing but is shown by arrows on a tree. Bear slightly left. Go ahead at another cross path to reach a stile out of the wood. *(0.4 mile)*

8 Over the stile, bear right across the corner of a field to another stile and on along the right-hand side of a field, over a lane and ahead along the right-hand side of a small field to a stile onto a concrete track. Turn right along the track to a lane and left along the lane for 150 yards. *(0.5 mile)*

9 Turn right on a signed path, the **Chiltern Way**. This soon becomes a superb path that descends through woodland, then terraces above **Stonor House**, before leading down to a road. *(1.2 mile)*

As you walk down this path you get a very good view of Stonor House, home of the Stonor family for over 800 years. It was built on the site of an ancient stone circle that you can see in front of the house. Parts of Stonor House are 11th century and the main house dates back to the 1400s. The Stonor family have always been devout Catholics. During the Reformation in the 16th century there was strong social and legal pressure on Catholics to forswear their faith, including heavy fines amounting to as much as £50,000 a year in modern money. Jesuit priests were sent secretly to England to co-ordinate and stiffen resistance. One of these was Edmund Campion, who was given refuge at Stonor Park. Campion lived secretly in attic chambers, and produced a pamphlet, titled *'Decem Rationes'* or *Ten Reasons,* an attempt to offer a logical appeal for why Catholicism was preferable to Protestantism. This high profile project proved his undoing: Campion was captured, and, under torture, made to confess where he had printed the work. He was hung, drawn and quartered at Tyburn. Stonor was raided on 4th August 1581, and the family had to pay a huge fine to regain their house and estate. John Stonor, who had invited Campion to his family home, was exiled for life to France. Stonor House is open to the public on Sunday afternoons in summer plus Wednesday afternoons in July and August. Telephone: 01491 638587.The estate is home to a herd of fallow deer, not always seen, that have grazed here since medieval times when the fragrant, thyme-flavoured, Stonor venison was much prized at Court.

⑩ Turn left along the road. Some 150 yards after a lane on the right, turn right on a footpath signed 'Maidensgrove'. Follow this up two fields, through a wood then across a third field. In the corner of this field follow the path between hedges to shortly reach a T-junction with a track. *(1.1 mile)*

⑪ Turn right for 30 yards, then left along a path for 20 yards and then right through a gate into **Warburg Nature Reserve**. Follow this path steeply downhill, ignoring a path to the right, to the lane leading to the reserve car park and turn right for a few yards back to the start. *(0.4 mile)*

Date walk completed:

THE WORMSLEY VALLEY

Where red kites soar

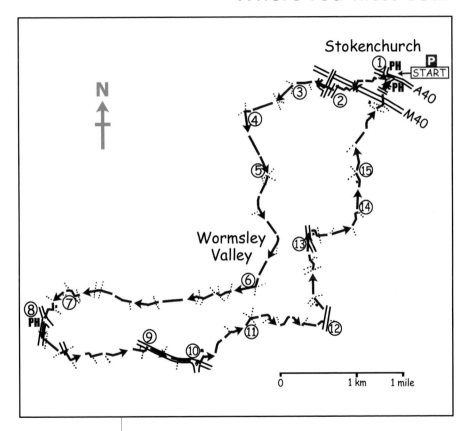

Distance:
10½ miles

Map: OS Explorer 171 Chiltern Hills West

Starting Point:
The Kings Hotel,
Stokenchurch.
GR: 760963

How to get there: *Stokenchurch is on the A40, the High Wycombe–Oxford road, just east of junction 5 on the M40. There is a public car park to the right of the Kings Hotel.*

A PASTORAL SCENE ALONG THE WAY

*T*he Chilterns has many delightful spots but queen of them all is the incomparable Wormsley Valley. The walking here is remarkably quiet for such an outstanding place because circuits centred round the Wormsley Valley tend to be quite long and involve significant climbing – just right for an adventurous walk to a good pub and this route was first on my list when I was planning this book. This may not be the longest route but it is certainly the most energetic with well over 1,000 ft of ascent. It is lovely at all times of year but the colours are breathtaking in autumn and there is a fine show of flowers in spring.

The **Fox and Hounds** at Christmas Common is believed to date back to the middle of the 17th century and has plenty of charm and character, from the roses round the door to the fire in the inglenook fireplace in the bar. A modern extension housing the restaurant has been built in the same style and does not detract. This is quite a foodie pub run by an award-winning chef but they are very happy to welcome walkers and serve sandwiches and ploughman's lunches as well as an extensive menu – or you could just choose one of their delicious starters if you want a lighter meal. The beer is Brakspear's.

Telephone: *01491 612599.*

Alternatives: The Four Horseshoes *(01494 485671)* and the Fleur de Lis *(01494 485671)* in Stokenchurch are both close to the car park where this walk starts.

 *The Walk*

1 Cross the main road and bear right across the common to meet a surfaced track. Turn left along the track past the cricket pavilion and some cottages then go over the M40 to reach a T-junction with a road. *(0.6 mile)*

Stokenchurch grew on the main London to Oxford road as a resting and changing place for horses. The Kings Hotel, which was the Kings Arms until it became a boutique hotel quite recently, was a coaching inn and Charles II is reputed to have stayed here. Its position on top of the Chilterns has its drawbacks: in the old days the parish was liable to water shortages and in the drought of 1870 beer was cheaper than water!

2 Turn left for 50 yards then right on a signed path along **Mill Lane**. Cross a road and continue along

Mill Lane, going over an access drive then shortly across a field to a fork. *(0.4 mile)*

3 Bear left into trees and maintain direction after 25 yards on the waymarked path, soon going steeply down to a drive. Cross the drive to a stile then bear slightly right uphill to a second stile and on through trees to a clear cross path just over the ridge. *(0.5 mile)*

This part of the Chilterns has become famous for its red kites and you are almost certain to see them on this walk. The red kite is a big bird with a wingspan of five feet. It has a distinctive forked tail, white flashes on its wings and bright yellow legs. These were once common birds and Shakespeare described London as 'a city of Red Kites and Crows': they were protected because they kept the streets free of carrion and rotting food. Their fortunes changed in the 16th century when an Act of Parliament for the

Preservation of Grain was passed. Red kites were included in a list of vermin species deemed to be a threat to food production and a bounty of one penny for every kite killed was paid in many parishes. This, combined with the activities of egg collectors, caused their numbers to drop and by the end of the 19th century red kites were extinct in England and Scotland, with only a few pairs surviving in the valleys of mid-Wales. In 1989, the Nature Conservancy Council and the RSPB launched a project to reintroduce the red kite back into England and Scotland. Kite chicks were brought into the Chilterns from Spain and released here on the Wormsley Estate. The first successful breeding in the Chilterns took place in 1992, and since then numbers have steadily increased to approximately about 400 breeding pairs and they are once again a common sight.

4 Turn left to reach a surfaced drive. *(0.5 mile)*

5 Turn right along the drive, ignoring turns to the right. When the drive turns right, signed 'To Cricket Ground', keep ahead on a track, which becomes a path when the wood on the right ends. Bear right to stay in the valley when this forks to reach a waymarked cross path, which is the **Chiltern Way**. *(1 mile)*

The American billionaire Paul Getty II bought the Wormsley Estate in 1984 and no expense was spared in its management, including planting some 90,000 trees. Though his first love was baseball, Paul Getty was introduced to cricket by Mick Jagger. He grew to love the game so much he had a cricket pitch constructed to first class standards, complete with thatched pavilion, where he invited teams, including touring test sides, to come to this idyllic setting to play his team.

6 Turn right over a stile. Head across a field to a drive then a second field to another drive. Turn right for 40 yards then left on a waymarked path. After 230 yards continue ahead as the **Chiltern Way** turns left then immediately cross a track to a somewhat incongruous urn on a pedestal. Keep ahead and follow this path as it climbs steadily through woods to a T-junction with a cross path just before the end of the wood. *(1.5 mile)*

7 Turn right to reach a fork after 100 yards. Take the left option (**path PY3**) to a T-junction with a track. Turn left. When the track ends at a house follow the grassy path to the right of the house on a fenced path, ignoring a path to the left, between fields to emerge at a road junction within the welcome sight of the **Fox and Hounds**. *(0.4 mile)*

This is Christmas Common. There are three explanations offered for the hamlet's unusual name. The first is that during the Civil War in 1643 the Royalist forces held the heights of the Chilterns while Cromwell's men were pitched down below in Watlington. That Christmas the opposing troops called a truce and met on the site of the pub to celebrate. The second story is that it originates from the large number of holly trees growing nearby. The third and most prosaic origin is from the name of a family with local connections.

8 Turn left and immediately fork right past the **Fox and Hounds**. Some 170 yards after the pub turn left on a path signed as the **Oxfordshire Way** and shortly continue ahead at a cross track. Follow this path through a wood to a track and turn left to almost immediately reach a lane. Turn right along the lane for 200 yards. Opposite the entrance to **Queen Wood Farm** turn left along a signed bridleway to continue on the Oxfordshire Way. As the path approaches the end of the wood, fork left, leaving the Oxfordshire Way, to follow a path just inside the wood. Ignore an unsigned path leading right then follow the waymarked path round to the right to reach a stile out of the wood. Continue along the right-hand side

of four small fields then for 60 yards along a track. When the track bends right, keep ahead through a small metal gate then follow the waymarked path round to the left to a lane. *(1.2 mile)*

9 Turn right. At a road junction keep ahead for 40 yards. *(0.5 mile)*

10 Turn left on a track to **Northend Farm**, soon entering the **Wormsley Estate** again. Follow the track downhill. At a pronounced left-hand bend bear right off the track, marked by a white arrow on a tree, and follow the path down to a drive. *(0.6 mile)*

As you walk down this path you have a great view over the Wormsley Valley – and of Stokenchurch telecommunications tower unfortunately looming over it. Erected in 1968, it is built of reinforced concrete and is 320 ft high.

11 Cross the drive and immediately go over a stile by a gate on the right. Head across a field to a second stile then follow the waymarked path between soaring beeches, shortly joining a wider path coming in from the right. Cross a narrow field then continue on the woodland path, soon climbing steeply, to a kissing gate near the top. Carry on over a field, along a hedged section and along a track to a lane. *(0.7 mile)*

12 Turn left for 150 yards then turn left on a signed path along a track. The track ends at **Far Side Cottage**: continue on the path ahead through trees, across a track and beside **Ibstone Common** (for more about Ibstone see Walk 8). Do not stray to the right across the common and at the far end of the open area do not follow the main path round to the right but carry on in the same direction into trees. Ignore a clear path to the left after 30 yards: this is the **Chiltern Way** joining our route and we follow it back to **Stokenchurch**. Continue for a further 100 yards to a fork. Take the left option and follow this path to emerge on a road. *(0.7 mile)*

13 Turn left for 180 yards then right through a small wooden gate immediately after **Mile House**. The path soon leads to a second gate as it has been diverted round the garden. Cross a track and follow the path ahead. Be careful to stay on the narrow waymarked path on the right rather than a wider path on the left as the latter soon turns left. Continue down into a valley to find a stile. Over the stile, turn left up the left-hand side of a field. Near the top of the field bear left back into the wood and continue climbing to a T-junction with a cross path. *(0.6 mile)*

14 Turn left, still on the **Chiltern Way**, to a stile by a gate then on up the left-hand side of two fields. Be sure to admire the ever-widening view behind as you climb – the valley you can see is explored by Walks 5 and 8. Cross a stile next to a field gate by a barn and continue ahead past farm buildings on a drive. *(0.3 mile)*

15 Immediately after passing through a gate, turn right over a stile then bear left across a field, passing to the right of a small copse, to a gate and stile in the far corner. Continue along the left-hand side of a field then down into a dip and up the other side towards a farm. Follow the waymarked path to the right of farm buildings across a field to a drive. Turn right then left under the M40. At the far end of the tunnel follow a surfaced track to the left then keep ahead along **Coopers Court Road** back to the centre of **Stokenchurch**. *(0.9 mile)*

Date walk completed:

IBSTONE, TURVILLE AND FINGEST

Three Chiltern villages

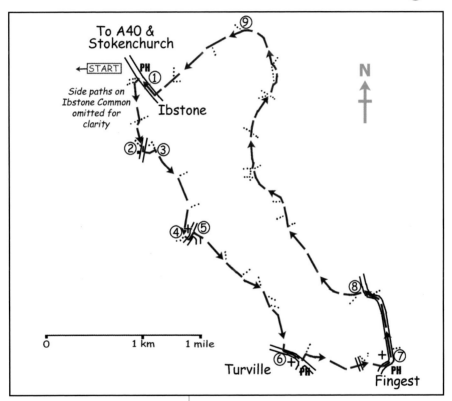

Distance:
7 miles

Map: OS Explorer 171 Chiltern Hills West

Starting Point:
Ibstone, where there is plenty of room to leave a car safely by the road near the Fox. The directions start from the Fox. GR: 751939

How to get there: *From the A40 just west of Stokenchurch take a minor road, signed 'Ibstone 2', over the M40 at junction 5 for 1½ miles to Ibstone. The Fox is on the left and there is roadside parking on the right.*

THE WINDMILL ABOVE THE VILLAGE OF TURVILLE

*T*hree villages mark the points of this route through one of the most beautiful parts of the Chilterns. Each has an ancient and interesting church as well as a pub so this circuit will therefore provide both physical and spiritual sustenance to the walker and you could view it as a pub – or church – crawl. One of the villages, Turville, may seem familiar even if you have never been there before as it is the backdrop to *The Vicar of Dibley*. Much of the route is through woods with some fields, commons and quiet lanes. At a bare seven miles, this charming walk is probably the easiest one in this book – ideal for a short winter day or a long summer afternoon, perhaps.

The **Bull and Butcher** in Turville is a quintessentially English pub in a location chosen for its charm. It was built as a house around 1550, but didn't sell alcohol until 1617 when workmen at the church threatened to lay down tools if no refreshments were provided. The owner began supplying ale and food for the workers, and the pub was born. It was apparently originally called the Bullen Butcher, referring to Henry VIII and Ann Boleyn or Bullen. Inside there are original beams and open fireplaces as well as one of Turville's wells, open to inspection in the Well Bar, having been uncovered when an extension was built in 2000. Outside there is a pleasant garden and patio. The food combines good pub grub with some exotic suggestions, such as lamb with Moroccan spiced taboulet. It is not surprising that the Bull and Butcher can be very busy indeed on summer weekends. The real ales include Brakspear's Ordinary, Oxford Gold Organic and Hooky Dark from Hook Norton.

Telephone: *01491 638283.*

Alternatives: The route starts at the Fox in Ibstone *(01491 639333)*, now more of a hotel and restaurant, and also passes the Chequers in Fingest *(01491 638335)*, which has a very large and attractive garden.

 The Walk

❶ With your back to the **Fox**, turn left along the road for 50 yards. Do not take a signed bridleway on the right but continue for another 5 yards to an unsigned path on the right, starting across planks over a ditch and leading along the right-hand side of **Ibstone Common**. After 25 yards bear left across the common, passing an upright stone* on the right, to a track. Cross the track to meet a cross path after 10 yards. Turn right then bear left at a fork after 20 yards and at a second after a further 50 yards to reach a track and a tiny lane. *(0.6 mile)*

* *This is known as the Millennium*

Stone and is a sarsen stone. They are found in many places in the Chilterns and are blocks of hard sandstone that may be the remains of the Reading Bed sandstone that once lay on top of the chalk.

❷ Turn right along the lane for 100 yards then turn left along a signed path opposite **Hell Corner Cottage**. Bear right downhill when the path forks 15 yards into the wood. *(0.1 mile)*

Ibstone straggles the road on top of a ridge. At first glance it appears to have no church, unusual in a village mentioned in the Domesday Book. In fact, the delightful little church with much Norman work stands a mile south of the village and is passed later on the route. It seems that over the centuries the centre of the village has shifted, leaving the church at an inconvenient distance. Legend has it that at one time an attempt was made to build a new church nearer the village. The Devil got to hear of it and took a dislike to the planned position. During the course of building he removed the structure so many times the builders finally abandoned the idea. Not surprisingly, the spot is now called Hell Corner.

❸ At the bottom of the hill the path meets a cross path. Turn right through the wood. The path climbs gently to reach a fork, indicated by the usual white arrow on a tree. Bear right and carry on along near the top of the slope until you reach a small church on the left. *(0.6 mile)*

❹ Turn left off the main path and walk through the churchyard to a lane. Turn left for 50 yards then right at a junction for 100 yards. *(0.1 mile)*

❺ Take a signed path on the left. Ignore a path on the left then bear right at a fork signed by a white arrow on a tree. Pass another path on the left and after a further 80 yards go over a stile on the right. Head towards **Turville**, seen nestling in the valley below, to find another stile to the right of a metal gate. Go

over the stile and follow the path down to a gate. Cut across the corner of a field to two more gates and on across a field to the road in Turville. *(1 mile)*

Turville must be the perfect English village – with pub, church and village green (and house prices to match). It has provided the scenery for numerous films and television programmes. The windmill above the village (see Walk 5) is a prominent landmark. Ellen Sadler was born in Turville in 1850 and was the tenth child of a family of twelve who lived in one of the small cottages. She was a normal, healthy child and at a young age was sent to Marlow as a nursemaid. She began to have symptoms of drowsiness and a pain in the head and was eventually sent to Reading Hospital. She stayed there for several weeks and was then returned home in a bed on a cart and proclaimed incurable. Even under her mother's care her condition deteriorated. On 29th March 1871 she said she could hear bells in her head and then went into convulsions. By the time the doctor arrived she had fallen into a sleep that was to last nine years. During this time she never once moved by herself. Her jaw was clenched but she was fed three times a day with port wine and sugar, using a small teapot.

THE BULL AND BUTCHER PUB

The liquid passed straight down her throat without any sign of swallowing. As time went by people came from far and wide to view the phenomenon. Among them were eminent doctors who, though full of medical terms, could come up with no cure or definite explanation. They rarely left without a tip for Mother. The local people were sceptical and suspected a fiddle. Nevertheless, it is hard to believe that a young girl would lie in one position without speaking or moving for nine years. And anyway, it must have cost a lot in port wine. In 1880 her mother died and one of her sisters took over her care. Whether it was due to the fact that her sister stepped up the doses of port wine to every hour and sometimes varied it with tea is not known, but Ellen's condition began to improve and she could soon sit up and talk. She could remember nothing of the time while she had been asleep and spoke and acted *like the child she had been when she went to sleep though she was now 21. She continued to live locally, married and had a substantial family.*

6 Turn left. Just before the **Bull and Butcher** turn left on a track, signed as the **Chiltern Way**, towards the windmill on the hill above. As the track enters a field, turn right through a wooden kissing gate. Cross the field to a stile then follow the path through more woodland, going over a lane. Bear right at a junction to reach **Fingest** and the **Chequers**. *(0.8 mile)*

The glory of St Bartholomew's is its massive Norman tower, which is some 60 ft high and 27 ft square. It has three storeys. The top one has the remaining bell of the original peal; the rest are supposed to have been lost in a bet between a previous rector and a colleague. The church is basically Saxon though the interior is much changed by Victorian restorers. No wedding in Fingest is supposed to be lucky unless the groom lifts the bride over the church gate. After a wedding the gate is locked to

make sure the custom is observed. I suppose a bad back is a small price to pay for a happy marriage.

7 Immediately after the church turn left along **Chequers Lane** for about ½ mile. *(0.5 mile)*

8 Turn left on a track through double metal gates on a signed path and bridleway. Just before it enters a field after about 80 yards, bear right and follow the path along the valley bottom, gently climbing all the way. When the bridleway turns left, continue ahead on the waymarked path. Go over two cross tracks to eventually join a track coming in on the left. Some 150 yards further on, the public right of way bears right, as shown by a white arrow on a tree then bears left to rejoin the main track. *(2.1 miles)*

9 Watch for white arrows and a sign on a tree warning of a fork '20 yds ahead'. Bear left, soon walking along the left-hand side of a field. At the end of the field, go ahead into woods. Press ahead at the top of the slope as the path leaves the wood to reach the road in **Ibstone**. Turn right back to the start. *(0.9 mile)*

Date walk completed:

BURNHAM BEECHES
The way through the woods

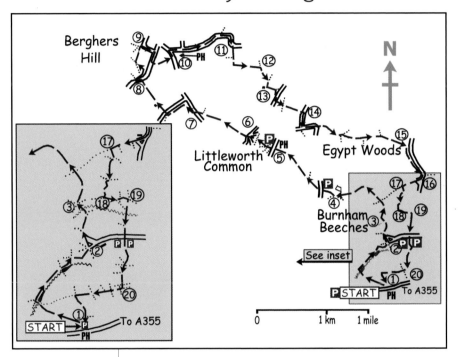

Distance:	Map: OS Explorer 172 Chiltern Hills East
9 miles	

Starting Point:
The public car park opposite the Stag, Burnham Beeches.
GR: 952843

How to get there: *At Farnham Common on the A355, the Beaconsfield–Slough road, turn along Beeches Road, signed 'Burnham Beeches 1'. At the crossroads turn left and follow this road for about a mile to the Stag on the left and the car park on the right.*

THE PUB AT POINT 10 OF THE WALK

*T*his lovely walk explores Burnham Beeches, over 500 acres of ancient woodland that are protected as a National Nature Reserve. The woods are beautiful at all times of the year and this walk is full of wildlife interest. It explores the less familiar Egypt Woods as well as the well known parts and leaves the Beeches to visit Littleworth Common and the surrounding area, where much of the walking is also through woodland. While not completely flat, there is no significant climbing so this is an ideal walk for a hot summer day when the trees shade the path and the sun brings out all the scents, particularly of the pines in Boveney Wood.

The **Royal Standard** at Wooburn Common has managed the retain a real pub atmosphere with excellent pub grub and ten real ales on offer, five from the hand pumps and five from barrels. There are plenty of tables outside, sadly overlooking a fairly busy road, but the beer and food make this an attractive refreshment stop. Interesting questions always arise during discussions at the pub and there is a range of reference books to resolve those knotty disputes.

Telephone: *01628 521121.*

Alternatives: The walk starts at the Stag *(01753 642226)* and passes the Blackwood Arms *(01753 642169)*, a Brakspear's house with a nice garden, soon after the start of the walk. Beeches Café at Burnham Beeches Visitor Centre sells cakes, snacks and hot drinks.

 The Walk

threw him in a pond and on another occasion he was left tied to a tree all night.

❶ With your back to the **Stag** and the road, take a path at the rear left of the car park to a pond. Walk past the end of the pond then turn right beside the pond then a stream (often dry) to a second pond. Continue ahead with this pond on the right then follow the path up to a cross path by a sculpture (if you reach a surfaced drive you have gone 20 yards too far). Turn right to emerge at **Victory Cross** with the visitor centre (toilets and café) a few yards ahead. *(0.6 mile)*

Burnham Beeches came on the market as land suitable for building 'superior residences' in 1879. Fortunately, the far-sighted naturalist Francis George Heath persuaded the Corporation of the City of London to acquire the land as a green lung for the city. This was not popular with the local residents, who resented the energetic management and flurry of by-laws introduced by the new owners. The first head keeper, Owen Arnett, had a very trying time. More than once angry locals

❷ Turn left, passing to the left of the noticeboard, to a gate across the drive. Some 15 yards after the gate bear right off the drive and follow the main path downhill, soon walking with a wire fence on the right. Some 40 yards after the fence ends turn left on a path that soon crosses a wooden bridge and heads uphill to a five-way junction after 45 yards. *(0.3 mile)*

I walk regularly in the Beeches and I often wonder if I will come across a body. Certainly it is statistically likely if you believe all you see on the telly. Several episodes of Midsomer Murders have been filmed here, as well as other television programmes and films, and it is not unusual to come across a film set. The use of the woods in this way is tightly controlled to protect them and the fees help pay the cost of management.

❸ Take the left-hand of two paths on the right and follow it to a drive at a junction. Continue ahead along

McAuliffe Drive, following it round as it swings left to a T-junction at a shelter. *(0.6 mile)*

Just because this area has been wooded from time immemorial, it doesn't mean that people didn't live here. On the right at the junction, marked by a plaque, is an earthwork variously called Hartley Court, Harlequin's and Hardicanute's Moat. An irregular moat, often full of water, surrounds an area of about one and a half acres with a continuous bank on the outside and dividing banks within. This is surrounded by a further bank and ditch enclosing about nine acres in all. Inside the inner moat is evidence of a house and a well. It is thought that the outer area was once cultivated for crops and the inner was the homestead. A fence to protect the cultivated land from deer and pigs grazing in the surrounding woods probably topped the banks. The date is uncertain but probably was the 12th to 14th centuries.

4 Turn right for 30 yards then fork right on a path that leads to a small car park and a lane. Cross the lane and continue ahead on a signed path through woodland then across a field and along the left-hand side of a second field to a lane and the **Blackwood Arms**. *(0.8 mile)*

5 Cross the lane and car park and continue on a path in the same direction to a fork after 50 yards. Bear right across **Littleworth Common**, ignoring all side branches to emerge at a road. *(0.2 mile)*

6 Turn right to a T-junction then left for 20 yards to a signed path on the right starting through a wooden kissing gate. Follow the fenced path to a road. *(0.5 mile)*

7 Cross the road into a wood and turn right on a permissive path just inside the wood, initially parallel with the road, to another road. Cross the road and continue along the **Beeches Way** on a surfaced track. When the track ends at a cottage continue in the same direction to a road. *(0.7 mile)*

8 Turn left for 90 yards then turn right through a gate into **Farm Wood**. Through the gate, turn immediately right, signed 'Mill Wood ¼ mile'. Bear right when the path forks then follow the main path as it turns left along the right-hand side of the wood to a cross path. Turn right to a T-junction then turn right again to a lane in **Berghers Hill**. *(0.5 mile)*

9 Keep ahead to a T-junction with a road. Turn right for 150 yards then left on a signed path and follow this through a wood to a road. *(0.4 mile)*

10 Turn left past the **Royal Standard** then take the first lane on the right. Follow this for a good ½ mile, round a right-hand bend. *(0.6 mile)*

11 When the lane bends left keep ahead on a signed path starting over a stile next to a field gate. Towards the far end of the field follow the path as it turns left across the field to a track. *(0.4 mile)*

12 Turn right. Follow the track past a farm. Immediately after passing through a gate across the track turn right to a road. *(0.3 mile)*

13 Turn right for 60 yards then turn left over a well-hidden stile into a wood. Press on ahead over a cross track to arrive at a lane. *(0.3 mile)*

14 Turn right to a T-junction. Turn left along **Boveney Wood Lane**, signed 'Burnham Beeches'. When the lane turns sharp right and changes its name to **Park Lane** continue in the same direction on a signed path along a track. This leads into a field: walk along the left-hand side of the field to a stile into a wood. Ignore a path on the right after 175 yards and go ahead for another 20 yards to a fork. Bear right. Ignore paths to right and left and press on to leave the wood and walk past some cottages to a road. *(1.2 mile)*

15 Immediately before the road, turn right on an unsigned path between a fence and the road. This runs parallel to the road and eventually reaches a cross track. Turn left to the road then right to continue along the road in the same direction for another 100 yards. *(0.3 mile)*

16 Turn right, passing some cottages, then, when the road ends, keep ahead along **Dukes Drive** for 230 yards, ignoring one major and several smaller paths on the left. *(0.2 mile)*

17 Watch for the stump of what would have been a magnificent tree on the right. Turn left opposite this, rising away from the drive. After 70 yards turn right and follow this path as it bears left after a few yards to reach a T-junction. Turn right and also follow this path round to the left so you are continuing in more or less the same direction to another T-junction. *(0.2 mile)*

Burnham Beeches has probably been wooded ever since the forest returned after the last Ice Age. This vestige of ancient woodland contains the largest collection of old beech trees in the world. Nearly all the old beeches have been pollarded, which has contributed to their longevity and given them the weird appearance we see today. A beech tree would ordinarily live for about 250 years but pollarding allows the tree to live for 400 years or more and grow into the gnarled giants for which Burnham Beeches is famous. Pollarding is an old form of woodland management. The trees were repeatedly lopped at head height to provide fuel and wood for small building jobs. This sounds brutal but the trees can sprout new growth safe from the animals that were allowed to graze the forest floor beneath. From the middle of the 19th century onwards, the use of wood as a fuel declined as coal became more readily available. There was no longer the same need to harvest a crop from the trees and pollarding declined. It is thought that at the end of the 18th century there were about 3,000 pollards in Burnham Beeches but now the number is down to just over 500. Many of the trees have not been cut for nearly 200 years. It is very important to conserve these old trees as they are a vital habitat for many tiny animals and there are very few places that have as many ancient pollards as Burnham Beeches. Old trees are being carefully re-pollarded to prolong their lives and a programme of cutting younger trees has started to provide the next generation of pollards.

18 Turn left. After 125 yards follow the main path as it bears slightly left, where a young tree is growing in the stump of an old giant, to reach a cross path after a further 100 yards and within sight of a road. *(0.1 mile)*

19 Turn right and walk down into a dip and up the other side to emerge on a surfaced drive with parking beside. Cross the drive and head across the open area opposite to find a path a few yards to the left on the far side. This is about 10 yards to the right of a bench. The path shortly leads to a small wooden gate next to a field gate. Go through the gate and follow the boardwalk ahead. When this ends, keep ahead over a cross path to a T-junction. *(0.5 mile)*

20 Turn right to a drive. Cross the drive and continue ahead for nearly ¼ mile to the second cross path, with a bench on the right. Turn left and this leads back to the car park where this walk started. *(0.4 mile)*

Date walk completed:

PENN
The American connection

PLAYING CRICKET ON THE GREEN AT PENN STREET

Distance:
8 miles

Map: OS Explorer 172 Chiltern Hills East

Starting Point:
Penn Street, where there are several spots where a car may be left without causing inconvenience. The directions are given from outside the Squirrel, the first of the pubs met on today's walk. GR: 923958

How to get there: *From the A404, the High Wycombe–Amersham road, about 2 miles west of its junction with the A413, take a minor road, Penn Street and signed 'Penn Street', to the village and the Squirrel on the left.*

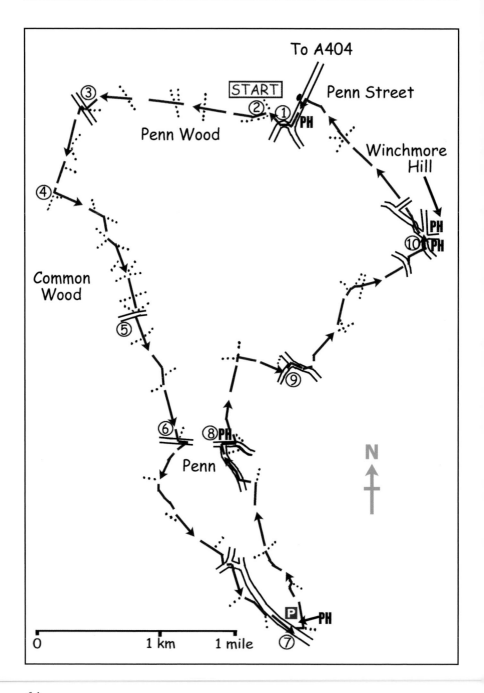

To A404

START

Penn Street

PH

Penn Wood

Winchmore
Hill

③

② ①

PH
PH
⑩ PH

④

Common
Wood

⑤

⑥

⑧ PH

⑨

Penn

N

P

PH

0   1 km   1 mile   ⑦

*T*his attractive walk is centred round the straggling village of Penn and is a must for those who enjoy woodland walking, as more than three-quarters of it is through some of the finest woods in the Chilterns. To refer to this route as a pub walk is perhaps not to do it justice as it can become more of a pub crawl, starting at one and passing four more.

This book would not be complete without the **Royal Standard of England** at Forty Green, which claims to be the oldest free house in the country and able to trace its history back to Saxon times. Its long and interesting past is recounted on the back of the menus. It is a fascinating old building with lots of nooks and crannies and plenty of tables outside, as well as a hitching post for horses. Until the 17th century it was called the Ship. The story goes that Charles I (or possibly the young Prince Charles) hid in the roof when he was on the run to France after the Battle of Worcester in 1651. After the Restoration, Charles II showed his gratitude by bestowing the unique name on the inn: there are plenty of pubs called the Royal Standard, one is visited on Walk 9, but only one Royal Standard of England. This deservedly popular pub features many traditional dishes on its menu such as mutton shepherd's pie and 'Buckinghamshire Bacon Badger', as well as sandwiches at lunchtime and tea and scones in the afternoon. They are keen to support local breweries such as Rebellion from Marlow, and stock a wide and interesting range of beers if you fancy something a bit different.

Telephone: *01494 673382.*

Alternatives: This route passes four other pubs. The Crown at Penn *(01494 812640)* is part of the Chef and Brewer chain so it is as much a restaurant as a pub. It has extensive gardens with a good view over the rest of this walk. Part of its old buildings was once a coffin-maker's. At the time of writing there are two pubs in Winchmore Hill, the Potters Arms *(01494 722641)* and the Furrow *(01494 721001)*, which until recently had always been known as the Plough. The Squirrel in Penn Street *(01494 711291)*, where this walk starts and finishes, is a delightful traditional pub and is home to Penn Street Cricket Club, which plays regular fixtures on the common opposite the pub throughout the summer, as well as a Boxing Day match against the rest of the village.

The Walk

❶ With your back to the **Squirrel** and facing the common, go left along the road to a junction and turn right, signed 'Penn 3 Beaconsfield 5'. When the road shortly bends left, turn right on a signed path into **Penn Wood** and follow the path ahead for 150 yards. *(0.2 mile)*

❷ Turn left through a wooden kissing gate. When the path forks after about 40 yards, take the right option. After a further 60 yards turn right on a wide path and follow this through the woods to a road. *(1 mile)*

Penn Wood is one of the largest ancient woodlands in the Chilterns. It has had many roles during its long history – as a hunting chase in Saxon times, as a pasture for commoners' pigs and as a source of wood sent via the Thames to London for use as fuel in the 14th and 15th centuries. It was used as a military training area in the mid 18th century and again in the Second World War. The right of local people to graze animals in the wood was extinguished by the Inclosure Award of 1855. It was probably at this time that several of the rides through the area were lined with specimen conifers and rhododendrons. The rhododendrons make a wonderful

display in May and June but are, of course, detrimental to the wildlife interest of the wood: few creepy crawlies live on them and they crowd out the native plants that should live beneath the trees. The management plan is to weed them out from most of the wood but leave them as a feature along the drives, such as this path. The woods faced a serious threat in 1993 when the then owners applied for planning permission for an 18-hole golf course. At first, it appeared that permission would be granted, and bulldozing the trees to clear fairways had begun before a determined campaign by local people persuaded the Secretary of State for the Environment to refuse planning permission, leaving the way clear for its purchase by the Woodland Trust.

❸ Turn right for 40 yards then left on a signed path into **Common Wood**. Follow this down into a dip and up the other side to a wide path on the left almost at the top (if you reach the end of the wood you have gone 50 yards too far). *(0.4 mile)*

Common Wood has a similar history to Penn Wood. The Inclosure Award of 1855 finally extinguished all rights of common in Penn, and from then on, Common Wood and Penn Wood became the private property of Earl Howe, whose descendant is still the local landowner. The dispossessed majority was outraged and seven years of active protest followed. Fences were pulled down in broad daylight, poaching was widespread and several people were sent to prison. In 2002, when Common Wood was put up for sale in 15 lots, Penn and Tylers Green Residents Society managed to raise enough money to buy Common Wood to secure it for local people. In effect, local people had to buy back what they had once freely enjoyed.

4 Turn left for ¼ mile. Turn right on an obvious path signed by a waymark (number 6) on a post for 130 yards. Turn left on a cross path. Follow the main path, bearing left at a fork by the number 7 waymark, to eventually arrive at a road. *(0.8 mile)*

5 Cross the road to continue in the same direction on a signed path 10 yards to the right. Follow the path up through woodland and out into a field. Keep ahead on a path to another road, in **Penn**. *(0.6 mile)*

The centre of the village is to the right. The name is Celtic and simply means hill, and Penn always had a reputation as a particularly healthy location. When various plagues affected London in the 15th and 16th centuries children were often sent to the area to enjoy the fresh air. Penn has a

place in American history through the family of that name. Sybil Penn was Lady of the Bed Chamber to the future Elizabeth I and Henry VIII gave her Penn House as a wedding present. Charles II named the American state of Pennsylvania in honour of Admiral Penn, who not only served loyally but also lent the king £16,000. William Penn, who lived from 1644 to 1718, was his son and the most famous member of the family. He became a Quaker at a time when they were a controversial sect and persuaded the king to give him the grant and charter of Pennsylvania to found a community based on Quaker principles. Penn's 'holy experiment' did not go well. His constitution proved unworkable, his principles were flouted and, from 1692, he was deprived of his powers as governor. Back in London, he lived in poverty in a house that was chosen for its convenience in getting away by water to avoid his creditors.

6 Turn left for 70 yards then right on a signed bridleway, part of the **Chiltern Way**, to a T-junction. Turn left again for about ½ mile. The path approaches a yellow metal gate. Some 50 yards before the gate bear right, as indicated by a blue arrow on a post, to emerge on a lane at a fork. Take the right branch of the fork downhill to a footpath starting over a stile on the right. Follow the footpath for about 250 yards to a cross path and turn left, downhill. The path approaches a lane and then runs parallel with it to a stile. Cross the stile and continue along the lane in the same direction as far as the **Royal Standard of England** a few yards along a track on the left. *(1.3 miles)*

7 Go to the right of the pub and immediately turn left on a signed path. A short hedged section leads to a gate into a field, then continues along the left-hand side of a field to another gate into a wood. Some 25 yards into the wood, the path reaches a T-junction. Turn left and follow the path through the wood to join a surfaced track after it leaves the wood. Walk along this for a good ¼ mile. Turn left over a stile onto a signed, fenced path leading to a lane. Turn right and carry on past **Penn church** to the main road. *(1.1 mile)*

The son of a churchwarden was a well known, not to say infamous, product of Penn. Jack Shrimpton was a notorious highwayman at the start of the 18th century, preying on travellers on the London to Oxford road near what is now Gerrards Cross. He is reputed to have taken as much as £150 in a day and ended his career on the gallows in 1713.

8 Turn right past the **Crown**. Turn left to the rear of the car park to find a path directly opposite five steps to the right of the building. Follow the path through a wood and then across a field to a wide cross path in the bottom of a dip. Turn right to a lane. *(0.7 mile)*

9 Turn left along the lane to a T-junction then right for 120 yards to a path on the left, again signed as the **Chiltern Way**. Follow this along the left-hand side of a field. At the end of the field turn right into a wood to a fork after 40 yards. Bear left to a surfaced drive and turn left along the drive to continue in the same direction for 275 yards. Now bear right off the drive on a waymarked path to a fork after 65 yards. Take the right option, soon leaving the wood. Press on across a field to a lane. Cross the lane and keep ahead along a signed bridleway along a track to emerge in the village of **Winchmore Hill** opposite the **Potters Arms**. *(1 mile)*

10 Turn left to the crossroads and the **Furrow**. Turn left, signed 'Wycombe', and walk beside the common. At a house called **Orchard Rise** leave the road and continue in the same direction towards a brick bus shelter. Cross a road and take a signed path opposite, to the right of some allotments. The path forks on leaving a wood at a metal kissing gate; take the right option and follow this to a track that leads to the road in **Penn Street**. Turn left back to the **Squirrel**. *(1.1 miles)*

WEST WYCOMBE AND HUGHENDEN
In Disraeli's footsteps

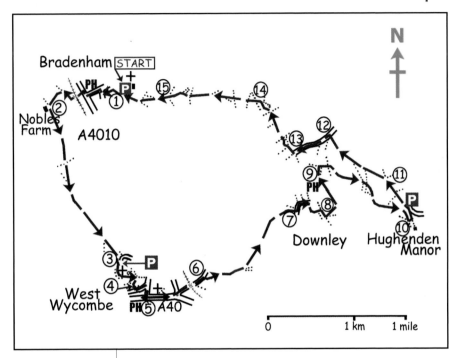

Distance:
8 miles

Map: OS Explorer 172 Chiltern Hills East

Starting Point:
The National Trust
car park at
Bradenham.
GR: 828970

How to get there: *From the A4010, the High
Wycombe–Aylesbury road, 1¾ miles north of its junction
with the A40, take a minor road signed 'Bradenham'.
Take the first lane on the right for 50 yards then turn
left on a track beside the village green to a car park.*

THE CHURCH AND MAUSOLEUM ABOVE WEST WESTCOMBE

I could have called this walk a tour of Chiltern des res as it passes three fine houses, Bradenham Manor, West Wycombe Park and Hughenden Manor, all in the care of the National Trust and the first and last associated with Benjamin Disraeli. It is a delightful walk, much of it in woodland but with some great views too and there is a lot to see along the way. West Wycombe Park and Hughenden Manor are both open to the public. It is also worth taking time to wander round the village of West Wycombe, also in the care of the National Trust, which is exceptionally picturesque with examples of many types of English architecture from the 16th century onwards.

The **George and Dragon** in West Wycombe is an old coaching inn on the road to Oxford. As you enjoy your pint, spare a moment to remember poor Sukie, a barmaid in the 18th century who fell in love with a rich gentleman. She received a note, apparently from her lover, asking her to meet him so they could elope. In fact the note was a cruel trick by the local lads. She turned up only to meet the lads teasing her, laughing and

70

throwing stones. One missile struck her on the head and killed her. Her ghost has been seen in the pub even in modern times. There is an atmospheric public bar (have a look at the clock behind the bar) with an open firplace and a large garden behind the pub. The full range of pub food is served at lunchtimes from sandwiches and ploughman's through to full meals including daily specials. The real ales at the time of writing show a fondness for Cornish beers and St Austell's Tribute and Sharp's Doom Bar, as well as the more usual Brakspear's Bitter and Courage Best,

Telephone: *01494 464414.*

Alternatives: There are two other pubs in West Wycombe – the Plough *(01494 538583)* and the Swan *(01494 527031)*. The Le De Spencers Arms *(01494 535317)* lies a couple of hundred yards off the route but is well positioned at Downley if you want to stop later in the walk. There is also an excellent tea room at Hughenden Manor *(01494 438638).*

 *The Walk*

Bradenham lies in a fold of the Chiltern hills and must come close to everyone's ideal of an English village with the manor house and church looking out across the green, complete with cricket pitch and surrounded by pretty cottages. It has been in the care of the National Trust since 1956. Bradenham Manor was rented by Isaac d'Israeli from 1829 until his death in 1848 while his famous son was rising to high office. It later became a boarding school and is now a residential training centre for a financial services company.

1 Walk back to the A4010 at the Red Lion. Turn right for 50 yards and then take a public footpath on the left through a metal kissing gate. Follow the path slightly left under the railway line then up the right-hand side of a small field and round to the right through a gate. Continue to a second gate. Some 25 yards after this gate bear left uphill to a T-junction with a track at **Nobles Farm**. *(0.6 mile)*

2 Turn left and follow the track along the ridge for about 1¼ miles to the car park on top of **West Wycombe Hill**. *(1.2 mile)*

3 Leave the path and walk across to the building with the golden ball on top. This is **St Lawrence's church**. Just past the church turn left to the **Mausoleum**. From the

Mausoleum follow the obvious path downhill towards **High Wycombe**, spread out at your feet. After 100 yards turn right down some steps. At the bottom of the steps turn left down towards **West Wycombe** to a lane. *(0.4 mile)*

This commanding hill was home to a settlement dating back to the Bronze Age; the Iron Age fortifications can be seen running parallel with the churchyard fence and at the eastern end are cut by the Mausoleum. This community grew into the Saxon village of Haveringdon. There was always a problem with water on this dry ridge so the population sensibly moved down into the valley and by the 19th century there were just two rate payers left living in Haveringdon. The church was rebuilt by Sir Francis Dashwood in the 18th century. The most unusual feature of all is the golden ball on top of the tower. It holds ten or twelve people and John Wilkes, a friend of Dashwood, described it as 'the best Globe tavern I was ever in'. The Mausoleum was inspired by the Coliseum in Rome and was part of the landscape design for West Wycombe Park. It contains memorials to members of the Dashwood family and their friends.

4 Turn left. Some 30 yards after the entrance to the **Hellfire Caves** bear right to shortly meet another lane. Turn right down into **West Wycombe**. The **George and Dragon** is a few yards to the right. *(0.2 mile)*

The path down the hill has an excellent view of West Wycombe House surrounded by its gardens and parkland. The Dashwood family acquired the West Wycombe estate in 1698 and still live there though the estate is owned by the National Trust. The house and grounds are open to the public on Sunday to Thursday in June, July and August from 2 pm to 6m and the grounds alone in April and May. Telephone: 01494 755571.

Francis Dashwood was a man of considerable energy, wealth and achievement, not to say profligacy. He became Chancellor of the Exchequer in 1762, said to be the worst ever at the time and he was widely held to be incapable of understanding a bar bill of five figures. Today his popular reputation is solely concerned with the Hellfire Club that met first at Medmenham Abbey and then in these caves. There were numerous Hellfire Clubs in the 18th century, set up by wealthy and aristocratic rakes to hold wild parties. Their reputation for drunkenness, sexual abandon and black magic became so notorious that they were banned. Dashwood's Apostles are perhaps remembered today because the political prominence of the members and exaggerated tales of the goings on were used as a political weapon at the time (see Walk 4). The caves, open at the weekend all year and every day in the summer, are not natural. They were dug to provide raw materials for the new road to High Wycombe that Dashwood built to relieve local poverty and unemployment.

5 Turn left (east) out of the village to a roundabout. Cross to **Cookshall Lane** to the left of a garage to continue in the same direction under the railway. Ignore a signed footpath on the right and continue for a further 100 yards to a signed bridleway on the right. *(0.5 mile)*

6 Turn right. At a three-way junction where the centre path goes up steps, take the left option and continue on the path to emerge on a lane in front of **Downley Common**. *(0.9 mile)*

7 Turn left and shortly follow the lane round to the right to a T-junction with a track. (The **Le De Spencers Arms** lies a couple of hundred yards along the track to the left.) Turn right. Follow the track round a left-hand bend, ignore a track on the right and keep ahead to the end of the track at a T-junction with a cross path. *(0.3 mile)*

8 Turn right through a wooden kissing gate and go ahead to a small gate near a stile. Through this gate, turn left then bear left at a fork after 15 yards to walk along the left-hand edge of the wood. After about ¼ mile pass to the left of a deep pit and keep ahead to a metal kissing gate out of the wood. *(0.5 mile)*

9 Do not go through the gate but turn right, steeply downhill, just before it. Cross a wide path at the bottom and continue, now in the National Trust **Hughenden Estate**, on this delightful path as it contours round the hillside through woodland. Ignore all side paths and follow the main path round to the right after just over ¼ mile then again round to the right after a further ¼ mile or so, following occasional white arrows and purple waymarks, to finally arrive at some steps on the left. *(0.8 mile)*

10 Go up the steps and across a small car park to a surfaced track. Turn left, passing the entrance facilities and tearoom (the house itself is to the right). Opposite the entrance drive, bear left along an unsurfaced track, signed 'Woodland Walk'. Follow this past the parking areas then ahead on a hedged track (not into the parking overflow field). *(0.4 mile)*

Disraeli loved the Chilterns and bought Hughenden Manor in 1848 for £35,000. He lived here for thirty-three years, until his death in 1881. Hughenden Manor was requisitioned by the Air Ministry during the Second World War. Codenamed 'Hillside', it was a top-secret intelligence and map-making facility involved in events such as the Dam Buster raids and D-Day landings. After the war, in 1946, the Air Ministry moved out and the property was made over to the National Trust. It is decorated as it might have been during Disraeli's time and is open to the public in the afternoons from Wednesday to Saturday and on Bank Holiday Mondays, 2 pm till 6 pm, between March and October and in December (telephone 01494 755565).

⓫ As the track bends slightly right, turn left through a small metal gate and follow the path half right across a field. At the far side keep ahead, initially with a wood on the left. Ignore paths to the left and press on to a lane. *(0.5 mile)*

⓬ Turn left. Continue along the lane when it becomes a track and round a right-hand bend as far as a left-hand bend. *(0.3 mile)*

⓭ This is **Naphill Common**. It is an open access area and a maze of official and unofficial paths. **If you**

reach a track or surfaced drive, you have strayed too far to the right and must go back and pick up the correct route. At the bend, keep ahead on an unsigned path to a fork after 25 yards. (This is essentially a walkers' path parallel to the official bridleway, which is very muddy and churned up by horses.) Bear left then left again after a further 30 yards. Now ignore all side turns and keep ahead on an occasionally waymarked path, bearing left yet again at an obvious fork. (If you reach the surfaced drive you have missed the fork by 25 yards.) After about ½ mile you should reach a post with waymarks showing a bridleway to the left. *(0.5 mile)*

⓮ Turn left (**not back on yourself on the bridleway you were shadowing**). Keep ahead on the bridleway, ignoring all side turns to reach a track after about ¾ mile. *(0.7 mile)*

⓯ Turn right to continue in the same direction. A gentle downhill stroll, taking the left option at a fork, leads back to the car park where this walk started. *(0.4 mile)*

Date walk completed:

AROUND GREAT HAMPDEN

John Hampden country

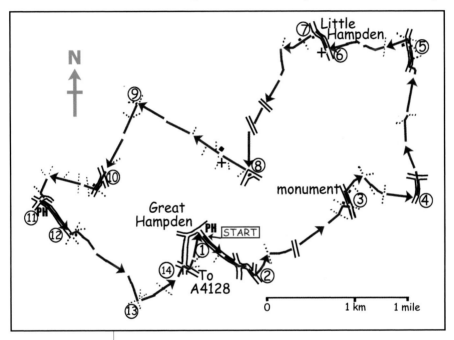

Distance:
9 miles

Map: OS Explorer 181 Chiltern Hills North

Starting Point:
Great Hampden
village hall and
cricket pitch.
GR: 846014

How to get there: *Take Hughenden Road (A4128) from High Wycombe. When this turns right to Great Missenden, continue ahead through Hughenden Valley for about a mile. Turn right along Warrendene Road for ¼ mile then go left on Bryants Bottom Road. Follow this for 2¼ miles. Turn right at a crossroads, signed 'Hampden ¾ Great Missenden 4'. Turn right at a T-junction then take the first road on the right, just before the Hampden Arms. Park near the village hall on the left.*

THE PINK & LILY PUB NEAR LACEY GREEN

*N*owhere in the Chilterns can be thought of as really remote but if anywhere warrants that description it is Great and Little Hampden, especially the latter, lost in a fold in the hills. Nonetheless, this corner of Buckinghamshire nurtured one of England's most notable Parliamentarians, the great John Hampden from whose family the villages take their names. His memorial, visited on this walk, looks out across a magnificent view of typical Chiltern scenery of steep-sided bottoms crowned with beech hangers. The first half is quite energetic with several ascents and descents as the route leads from Great Hampden to Little Hampden and then to the family seat of Hampden House. The second half from there to the famous Pink & Lily pub is more level and, in common with the first part of the walk, offers much enjoyable woodland walking.

 The **Pink & Lily** is positioned about two-thirds of the way round this walk, in Parslows Hillock. Just when you feel in need of some refreshment, there it is! As well as Braksprear's, two guest beers are offered, favouring local breweries such as Marlow's Rebellion. It serves excellent food – snacks such as filled jacket potatoes and sandwiches, as well as full meals. It is much altered since Rupert Brooke visited it whilst walking in the Chilterns in 1913. He wrote some lines of doggerel about the place and these are displayed in the Brooke Bar, which is kept much as the pub was in his day. It is decorated with photos of the poet and his grave, a corner of a foreign field forever England.

Telephone: *01494 488308.*

Alternatives: The Hampden Arms *(01494 488255)* is very close to the end of the walk or, of course, you could visit it first. It has been a pub since 1915 and the first licensee was the Earl of Buckingham. He didn't run it himself, of course. It was managed by the People's Temperance Society – the mind boggles! They offer a wide selection of full meals, as well as light lunches.

The Walk

Great Hampden was the ancestral home of the Hampden family since before the Norman Conquest. After twenty-four generations as lords of the manor, the family became extinct in the male line in 1754 and the estate was left to a cousin, who took the name Hampden. The last member of the family to live in the ancestral home organised the laying of the immaculately maintained village cricket pitch in 1950. When he died his memorial was an extension to the village hall, incorporating committee room, entrance and pavilion.

❶ Facing the cricket pitch, go left along the lane. Continue ahead at a junction to the next junction. *(0.4 mile)*

❷ Take a signed path on the left and follow this through a small patch of woodland then initially along the right-hand side of a field. When the wood on the right ends, bear slightly left across the field then continue with a hedge on the right. Keep ahead as the path enters woodland to a lane in a dip. Cross the lane and carry on up the other side. Shortly follow the path round to the left into a field then along the right-hand side of two fields. At the end of the second field go over a stile ahead and follow the path towards buildings. Turn right in front of the buildings to a stile onto a lane. *(0.9 mile)*

3 Turn left along the lane for 200 yards to a monument on the right commemorating the life and work of John Hampden, overlooking a wonderful panorama of Chiltern countryside. Take a signed path on the right immediately after the monument and follow this across a field to a stile into a wood. Carry on along the path just inside the wood for about 200 yards to a cross path. Turn right for 140 yards then turn left. Keep ahead over a cross path to soon leave the wood and walk along the left-hand side of a field and then between hedges to a lane. *(0.7 mile)*

John Hampden was an MP in the turbulent years leading up to the Civil War. He was a leader of the revolt against tax demands by Charles I, which he maintained were illegal unless approved by Parliament, and consequently spent periods in gaol. For example, his estate was assessed to pay 20 shillings' Ship Money, ostensibly demanded to finance an attack on France, and he refused to pay. Hampden's greatest skill in the stormy sessions of Parliament at this time was as a tactician and moderator, often defusing volatile situations and winning over his opponents by subtle persuasion. He was admired as a gentleman of honour and integrity by all parties. Hampden was one of the five MPs accused of treason whose arrest was demanded by the king in January 1642. He declared that there were two conditions under which active resistance to the king became the duty of a good subject: an attack upon religion and an attack upon the fundamental laws of the land and he had no doubt that King Charles I had fulfilled both these conditions. John Hampden was killed early in the conflict at the Battle of Chalgrove on 18 June 1643. This was a great loss as he was an important moderating influence on the Puritan side. A gruesome footnote is that his body was exhumed from the churchyard in 1828 to settle an argument about whether he was killed by gunshot wounds or the explosion of his own pistol. The discovery of an arm wrapped in a separate cloth suggests the latter.

4 Turn left down to a road. Cross the road to a stile and path that continues in the same direction up the other side to join a rough track coming in from the left. When the track bends right after a few yards, keep ahead on a path along the left-hand side of a wood and maintain this direction when the path leaves the wood to reach a lane. Turn right along the lane, little more than a track, to **Cobblers Hill Farm**. *(1.1 mile)*

5 Turn left on a track that appears to be an entrance drive. (If you reach a cross track and a post festooned with waymarks you have gone 25 yards too far.) The track becomes a path after passing farm buildings and soon enters a wood: follow it downhill and out of the wood and up the other side to reach a lane at **Little Hampden church**. *(0.6 mile)*

6 Turn right along the lane. *(0.2 mile)*

7 Turn left on a track immediately after a house called **Oaklands**. Keep ahead when the track ends at **Warren Cottage**, soon entering woodland. Watch for white arrows on a tree marking a T-junction and turn left. Follow the path through the wood and then down the left-hand side of a field to a road. Cross the road and continue on the path to a second road. Go over this road to a signed path 15 yards to the left and follow this uphill from stile to stile to a surfaced drive to **Hampden House and church**. *(1.2 mile)*

Hampden House, seen to the right, was the home of the Hampdens for centuries. The present building dates mainly from the 16th century, though there are traces of earlier structures. In the 20th century it was the headquarters of Hammer House horror films and frequently used as the setting for their productions. Today it is an insurance company's offices.

8 Turn right through a gate and walk along the drive past the church and **Hampden House**. Continue ahead through a gate when the drive shortly ends and ignore a path over a stile on the right. Go through a second gate and ahead a few yards to a track. Turn right. When the track bends right, leave the track and continue ahead for 40 yards. The footpath and bridleway now diverge and it is much more pleasant to walk on the footpath just inside a wood. Eventually a wire fence bars the way ahead through the wood. Go left to rejoin the bridleway and continue in the same direction, either on the bridleway or the adjacent path, through woodland for about 300 yards to a cross path. *(0.9 mile)*

9 Turn left. Ignore a track on the right and press ahead along the right-hand side of a field. At the end of the field, re-enter woodland and follow the path to emerge at a road junction. *(0.5 mile)*

As you approach the road you will notice that you are walking on a prominent bank and you may have seen others in the woods. This is part of Grim's Ditch. This system of banks and ditches is found erratically in many parts of southern England. It was certainly not built by an unknown Grim and the different parts may not even have much to do with each other. Some are Iron Age while other bits may be as late as the Saxon period. While it is shrouded in a certain amount of mystery, its structure suggests it was not a defensive fortification and was probably a boundary marker.

⑩ Take the lane ahead, signed 'Lacey Green 2', for about 200 yards. Immediately after a house on the right, turn right and follow the waymarked path through the woods, ignoring all unsigned cross paths and side turns to eventually arrive at a stile and a cross path. Turn left. At a track turn left again to a road. Turn right to the **Pink & Lily**. *(0.7 mile)*

I have heard two theories as to how the Pink & Lily acquired its distinctive name. The first, and more romantic, says that a Miss Lily, parlour maid at Hampden House, married Mr Pink, butler, and they opened a pub that took their names. The more prosaic explanation says what else would you call a pub at the junction of Pink Road and Lily Bottom Lane?

⑪ Immediately before the pub turn left along **Lily Bottom Lane** for a good ¼ mile. *(0.3 mile)*

⑫ Just before the surface ends, turn left along a track signed as a public bridleway, passing an attractive cottage on the right. At the end of the cottage turn right along the first path on the right and walk just inside a wood to an obvious cross path with wooden railings. *(0.7 mile)*

⑬ Turn left. After 25 yards go through a gap in the fence on the left to walk parallel with the much muddier bridleway on the right. The Hampden Estate is to be congratulated for creating footpaths parallel with bridleways, which can be unpleasant churned up by horses. Follow the waymarked path to a crossroads. *(0.4 mile)*

⑭ Turn right, signed 'Hughenden 3 High Wycombe 5½', for 45 yards. Turn left. The path forks immediately: take the left branch ahead for 75 yards to a second fork and take the left option again. This shortly leads to a stile onto the cricket pitch. Go ahead, back to the village hall. *(0.3 mile)*

Date walk completed:

COOMBE AND WHITELEAF HILLS
Roaming the Ridgeway

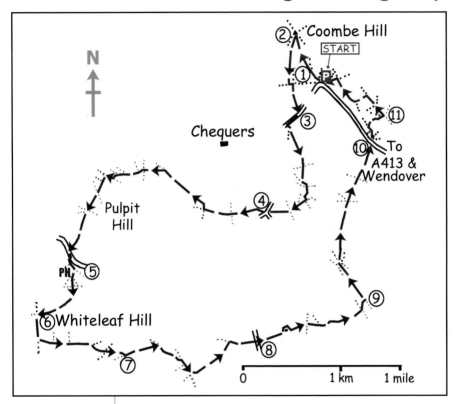

N↑

②↖ Coombe Hill
START
① P
③
Chequers
⑪
⑩ To A413 & Wendover
④
Pulpit Hill
PH ⑤
⑥ Whiteleaf Hill
⑨
⑦
⑧
0   1 km   1 mile

Distance: 8 miles	**Map: OS Explorer 181 Chiltern Hills North**
Starting Point: Coombe Hill car park. GR: 852062	**How to get there:** *From the A413, the Wendover–Amersham road, about a mile south of Wendover take a minor road west, Dunsmore Lane, signed 'Dunsmore 1'. Keep ahead at all junctions for just less than 2 miles to a car park on the right on a sharp left-hand bend.*

THE COOMBE HILL MONUMENT

*T*he scarp slope of the Chilterns on the northern side of the hills rises up steeply from the Vale of Aylesbury below and has some of the best viewpoints. This superb walk visits two of them, Coombe Hill and Whiteleaf Hill, using the long-distance Ridgeway to connect the two, from which there is a succession of sweeping panoramas. A clear day is a must to get the best from this highly recommended walk. The route also skirts Chequers, the country house provided for the use of the Prime Minister. The return is mainly, though not entirely, through beautiful and varied woodland, carpeted with a fine show of bluebells in many parts in May.

Dating back to the 16th century, the **Plough** at Lower Cadsden was once a staging post for coaches between London and Thame and is one of the oldest pubs in the area. In 1643 John Hampden's cortège paused here to hold a wake whilst escorting his body back to the family home at Great Hampden from Thame, where he died following the Battle of Chalgrove (see Walk 12). The Chilterns was once famous for its cherry orchards and the

Plough hosted the annual Cherry Pie Festival, which had been celebrated for generations to mark the end of the cherry season and has recently been revived on the first Sunday in August. As one of the few pubs on the Ridgeway, the Plough is very popular with walkers and has lots of tables outside. The full range of food from sandwiches through snacks to full meals is available.

Telephone: 01844 343302.

Alternatives: There are no other pubs or other sources of refreshment on this walk.

 The Walk

1 Return to the lane and go through a gate on the right to a National Trust information board. Follow the path ahead to the monument on **Coombe Hill**. *(0.4 mile)*

Coombe Hill is 852 ft above sea level. It is the highest viewpoint of the Chilterns but it is not the highest point. That lies three miles away in Wendover Woods and is visited on Walk 15. The monument, erected in 1904, is to 148 soldiers who died in the Boer War. It was almost totally destroyed by lightning in 1938 and was rebuilt the same year and again badly damaged by a lightning strike in the early 1990s taking several months to repair so it has now has been equipped with conductors to prevent the mishap happening again.

2 At the monument turn left, back on yourself but at a slightly lower level on the **Ridgeway**, signed with the white acorn long distance trail waymark. The route now follows the Ridgeway along the escarpment to the top of **Whiteleaf Hill** (point 6). Follow the level path, ignoring all paths leading downhill to the right. Continue on the Ridgeway through a metal kissing gate to a lane. *(0.5 mile)*

The Ridgeway is one of the great trade routes of England. It has probably been in use for 4,000 years and is one of the oldest roads in the world. It leads from the Dorset coast to the North Sea and rides the back of one of the six great ridges that radiate from Salisbury Plain. It is thought that this ancient route followed the high chalk land to avoid thick forest and marsh, and prehistoric remains are found in abundance.

Keeping company with the Ridgeway for some of its length is another ancient highway, the Icknield Way, though it came into being later. The Ridgeway, being on top of chalk hills, had no water, which is why there are no villages on it today. The Icknield Way runs nearer to the spring line so giving travellers easier access to water. When it came into use there were, presumably, fewer dangers from wolves and other wild animals in the woods. It is still very old and has an older name than the Ridgeway. The latter is what its name implies in modern English and the word comes from the Anglo-Saxon 'hryeg', meaning ridge. Icknield is a name so old it has no known root and must embody some term from a long forgotten tongue. The Ridgeway Path is a modern creation that runs from Ivinghoe Beacon in Buckinghamshire to Overton Hill in Wiltshire. In part it follows the line of the ancient Ridgeway but also uses other paths.

3 Turn right for 150 yards then left on a track for 20 yards. Go over the second stile on the right and follow the **Ridgeway** through magnificent mature beech woods to a T-junction. Turn right and walk downhill, going over a broad cross path, to a road. *(0.9 mile)*

4 Cross the road and continue along the **Ridgeway**, passing **Chequers** to the right. Cross the driveway and keep ahead over a field to a gate. Through the gate, turn right, still on the Ridgeway. Through the next gate, keep ahead, ignoring faint paths forking left and right, to reach another gate and a cross path. Press on ahead downhill then round the hill, bearing left at a fork to a sunken cross path. Turn right for 30 yards then left to continue on the Ridgeway. Go down into a dip and up the other side, ignoring branches on the left until you come to a wooden gate. The path is contouring along the side of **Pulpit Hill**. Press on over a crossing path to follow a path downhill. When the path forks, the left-hand branch is the drier footpath, the right is a bridleway, which can be very muddy. At a road turn left to the **Plough**. *(1.7 mile)*

There has been a house on the site of Chequers since the 12th century but the building we see today dates from the 16th century. It had the dubious honour of guarding a royal prisoner, the unfortunate Lady Mary Grey, who was described as the smallest person at court, crooked backed and very ugly. In the turbulent times following the death of Henry VIII, she had some claim to the throne but never made a serious attempt. She was imprisoned in 1565 for marrying without the permission of Queen Elizabeth I and was kept confined to ensure that, in the words of that great virgin Queen, 'there were no little bastards'. She languished at Chequers for two years, although probably not in too much discomfort. In the early 20th century the house was owned by Arthur Lee, the Tory Minister of Agriculture, who decided to give it to the nation as a country retreat for the prime minister. While previous prime ministers had always belonged to the landed gentry, the post-First World War era saw the rise of politicians of more humble origins who did not have the country houses of previous prime ministers to entertain foreign dignitaries, or a tranquil place to relax from the affairs of state. As Stanley Baldwin said: 'There are three classes that need sanctuary more than any others: birds, wildflowers and prime ministers.' Chequers is a refuge and no prime minister, however socialist, has ever failed to succumb to its charms.

THE PLOUGH INN AT CADSDEN

5 Turn right on the **Ridgeway** just beyond the **Plough**. After 50 yards bear left to a gate into a beech wood. When the path splits, take the right-hand branch and follow the Ridgeway steeply uphill to the summit of **Whiteleaf Hill**. At the top the trees give way and for the best view go to the edge of the escarpment where there are information panels and seats to enjoy the panorama. *(0.5 mile)*

Cut into the side of Whiteleaf Hill is Whiteleaf Cross. It has a triangular base and arms nearly 23 ft wide, with a span of over 83 ft. Like the nearby Bledlow Cross, its origins are obscure but as a charter of AD 903 refers to a boundary mark here, it is likely to be of ancient origin. It cannot really be seen when you are

85

standing above it. The 'monument' seen in the distance is the telecommunications tower near Stokenchurch.

6 Continue on the **Ridgeway** from **Whiteleaf Hill** for about 130 yards to a signed bridleway on the left. Turn left, leaving the Ridgeway. Follow the path for a good ¼ mile to a fork. Bear right on a rising path to a cross path. Go over this and carry on in the same direction to a T-junction. *(0.7 mile)*

7 Turn left. Continue ahead as a path joins from the left to reach a stile onto a drive. Turn right and walk along the drive to eventually reach a road. *(1 mile)*

8 Cross the road and continue in the same direction, now on the drive to **Hampden Chase**. As the drive approaches the house, turn left on a permitted path round the garden to avoid invading their privacy then follow the path into a wood. When the path forks about 40 yards into the wood, bear right and carry on along the path out of the wood into a field. Turn right along the right-hand side of the first field and the left-hand side of a second. At the end of the second field continue ahead into a wood, soon passing a massive, gnarled tree, to a T-junction after 100 yards. *(0.8 mile)*

9 Turn right for 20 yards then left on a path signed, among many on a waymark post, as the **South Bucks Way**. Follow this to a crossing track. Go over the track. Of the two paths ahead take the one on the right, still the South Bucks Way, and after 10 yards fork right on a path that, initially, runs quite close to the right-hand side of the wood. Press on down into a dip, over a cross path and up the other side then down again to a lane. *(1 mile)*

10 Cross the lane to a stile and, over the stile, turn immediately left and follow this up to join a path coming in from the left. Keep on the main path as it shortly bears round to the right and follow it to a stile onto a wide path. *(0.2 mile)*

11 Over the stile turn left for 300 yards, crossing a broad path after 150 yards. At a junction marked by a yellow arrow on a post turn left for 200 yards. At a T-junction turn right. Ignore several unmarked side turns and cross paths and continue for 300 yards until you come to a waymarked cross path. Turn left and follow the path to the car park where this walk started. *(0.5 mile)*

Date walk completed:

GREAT MISSENDEN AND WENDOVER

Above the Misbourne Valley

THE COTTAGE PASSED AT POINT 14 OF THE WALK

Distance:
11 miles

Map: OS Explorer 181 Chiltern Hills North

Starting Point:
Great Missenden
car park, Link
Road (charge
except on
Sunday).
GR: 894014

How to get there: *Great Missenden lies just off the A413,
the Amersham–Wendover road. The car park is on the right
of the road linking the main road (the A413) to the village.*

87

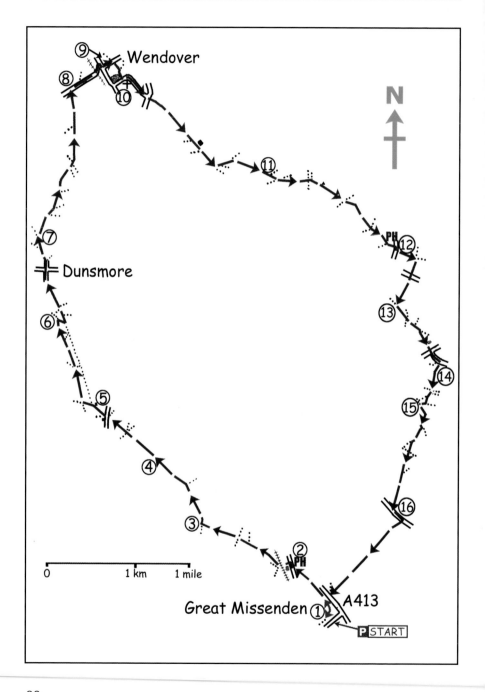

This route explores both sides of the Misbourne Valley between Great Missenden and Wendover, though you will be lucky to actually see the elusive river. The outward leg is an exhilarating ridge walk with some fantastic views and is fairly level after the initial climb. The return on the other side of the valley is less dramatic and includes long stretches of very attractive woodland walking. Towards the end of the walk there is an excellent view of Great Missenden in the valley below and the ridge explored at the start.

The **Old Swan** at Swan Bottom is a charming 16th-century freehold pub with a wealth of exposed beams and a welcome open fire in winter. There is a large garden where it is pleasant to sit and rest in the summer. Their two permanent beers are Brakspear's Bitter and St Austell's Tribute and they also offer two guest ales that vary according to season or availability, with a preference for locally brewed guest beers. The food is good, unpretentious pub grub, supplemented at lunchtime by a selection of sandwiches and filled jacket potatoes. Please note that the Old Swan is closed during the day on Monday.

Telephone: *01494 837239.*

Alternatives: The featured pub is reached quite late on the route and so if you wish to call there at lunchtime you will have to make an early start. The Black Horse at Mobwell *(01494 862537)* is passed soon after the start of the walk and has the distinction of being home to a ballooning club. An alternative for a pub lunch, and to visit the centre of Wendover, is to turn left at the end of point 8. This soon reaches the King and Queen *(01296 623272)* on the right or in the centre of Wendover, to the right, is the old coaching inn, the Red Lion *(01296 622266)*. Records date it back to 1670, although it is likely to be very much older. Oliver Cromwell is said to have stayed in 1642. Robert Louis Stevenson visited in 1875 and admired the wood panelling in the parlour.

 *The Walk*

❶ Go to the rear of the car park and turn right on a path in front of high railings. Continue through a gate and bear round to the left to a second gate. Press on across a field, soon walking by a channel, which is the bed of the **River Misbourne**. Keep to the right of this to find a stile about 50 yards from the far right corner of the field. Bear slightly left across the next field towards the **Black Horse** pub and a road. *(0.5 mile)*

The Misbourne is a winterbourne – a river that only flows when the water in the underlying aquifer is high enough to reach the surface. The river has been severely affected by over-abstraction and you will be lucky to see any water. The channel across the field is quite distinct and there are historical records of the river being thirty feet wide here. It is thought to have changed its course more than once, and you can see traces of other channels in this field, each change being said to presage a national disaster! A pond on the left at * below, which may be dried up, is said to be the source of the Misbourne. However, it has been known to rise above this point at Rignall Farm and there are records of the farm kitchen having to be pumped out before the First World War.

2 Turn right for 40 yards then turn left on a signed footpath*. Go straight ahead under the railway to a stile. Over the stile, bear right to the right-hand one of two visible stiles. Cross

the next field on a very well defined path to some steps at the far end. At the top of the steps continue up in the same direction and at the end of the field follow the path through a wood. *(0.8 mile)*

3 At a T-junction at the end of the wood turn right. Follow the hedged path then press on along the left-hand side of a field. Ahead right is an excellent view of **Wendover Woods**, which is the highest point of the Chilterns (see Walk 15). At the far side of the field continue on into a wood, ignoring a path on the right. *(0.5 mile)*

4 At the end of the wood continue on a path between hedges. This may sometimes be very muddy. If so, it can be avoided by taking a parallel path over a stile in the fields on the left. Cross a track and then a road at **Cobblers Hill Farm** and continue in the same direction. After 150 yards the track ends at a house called **Colenso**. *(0.6 mile)*

5 Cross a stile on the left and cut across the corner of the small field to another stile. Over this, continue in the same direction across a field to a stile partway along the fence opposite. Cross the stile and after 75 yards turn right along a crossing path. Follow this as it contours along the hillside with magnificent views on the left for a good ½ mile to a stile. *(0.7 mile)*

6 Do not cross the stile but turn sharp right, almost back on yourself, and go gently uphill to a track. Turn left. Cross a lane and continue along the lane opposite into **Dunsmore**. Walk through the village. Continue past the last house, ignoring a path bearing left, to a fork. *(0.7 mile)*

7 Take the right option, soon following a fenced path between fields then down through woods, ignoring a path through a gate on the right. When the way forks, shown by a waymark on a tree, bear left, still downhill. Continue on the path as it swings slightly left and uphill, as directed by a waymark. Ignore two paths on the right as the path bends left to eventually arrive at a stile out of the wood. Over the stile, head half left across a field to a second stile and press on in the same direction, now uphill to a metal kissing gate. Maintain direction on a fenced path, ignoring a path on the left, to a lane. *(1.1 mile)*

8 Turn right to the main road. (Turn left along the main road if you wish to go into the centre of **Wendover** for a pub lunch or to visit the town.) *(0.3 mile)*

Wendover is a very ancient town first mentioned in a will in AD 970 but it is certainly older than that as it is strategically situated at the entrance to one of the gaps through the Chilterns and the High Street is on the line of the Icknield Way. It is worth wandering round Wendover as there are many old buildings that appear to have hardly altered over the years, including the Red Lion.

9 Turn right for 50 yards then left on **Chapel Lane** for 170 yards. Immediately after a children's playground turn right. At a T-junction with a surfaced path (the **Ridgeway**) turn right, soon passing a pond on the right, to emerge opposite a church. *(0.3 mile)*

10 Turn left. As the road bends left continue in the same direction on the **Ridgeway** along an initially surfaced drive and follow this gently uphill for ½ mile, ignoring all side turns, past **Boswells Farm** on the left, to a footpath junction at the entrance to a wood. Bear left to stay on the Ridgeway. Ignore an uphill path on the right after 25 yards and continue on the level path for a further 125 yards to a path junction. Bear right uphill, still on the Ridgeway, for a good ¼ mile to a junction near the top of the rise (if the path starts going downhill, you have gone about 50 yards too far). *(1.3 mile)*

11 Bear right, leaving the Ridgeway, and at the top of the slope turn left onto a broad cross path. Follow this path, ignoring a left fork almost immediately, for ¼ mile to a cross path. Continue ahead, soon passing a concrete Ordnance Survey trig point. Ignore all side turns and press on, always in the same direction, to eventually arrive at a lane and the **Old Swan** on the left. *(1 mile)*

The map shows this trig point to be 761 ft above sea level. Mapping by triangulation requires clear lines of sight to other features so this was presumably an open hillside when the original survey was done. A glance around will support this idea as all the trees are young with none of the gnarled old giants found in some other parts of the Chilterns.

12 Turn right along the lane for 20 yards past the drive to **Kingswood House** then turn left over a stile on a signed path. At the end of the field go over a stile onto a cross path and turn right down to a lane. Cross the lane and continue on the path, starting along the drive to **Kingsvale Farm**, and follow this to a gate onto a cross path. *(0.5 mile)*

13 Turn left. When the path emerges into a field, bear right to a road junction in **The Lee**. Take the road ahead, signed 'Lee Common'. Ignore a signed path on the right just before the school and go ahead a few yards to a second path just after the school. *(0.5 mile)*

14 Turn right. The track soon leads to a gate into a field. Bear slightly left to a gate in a dip and, through the gate,

go ahead on a track for 80 yards. Bear left on a waymarked path across a field to a gravelled track and turn right to a T-junction with a cross track. *(0.4 mile)*

15 Turn left to the end of the track, where there are gates and a seat. Immediately after the seat, go over a stile by a metal gate and walk along the right-hand side of a field for 200 yards. As the hedge bears right, bear slightly left across the field to a stile. Continue in the same direction over three fields to a road. *(0.8 mile)*

16 Turn left for 175 yards. Turn right on a public footpath along a tarmac drive to a gateway then keep to the left of the gate and follow an enclosed path to a kissing gate into a field ahead. Go ahead downhill with views over **Great Missenden** in the valley below to a road. Cross the very busy A413 to a stile on the other side of the road. Bear left to rejoin the outward route back to the car park where this walk started. *(1 mile)*

Great Missenden is famous today as the home of the author Roald Dahl who lived and wrote here for 36 years until his death in 1990 when his family gave him a 'sort of Viking funeral', according to his granddaughter. He was buried with his snooker cues, some very good burgundy, chocolates, HB pencils (he always wrote in pencil) and a power saw.

CHOLESBURY AND WENDOVER WOODS

To the summit

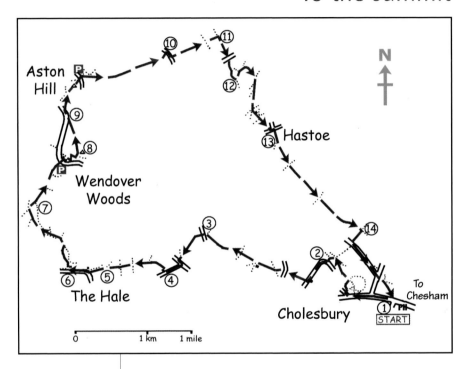

Distance:	Map: OS Explorer 181 Chiltern Hills North
10 miles	

Starting Point: **How to get there:** *From the A416, the*
The Full Moon, *Chesham–Berkhamsted road, at the north end of Chesham*
Cholesbury.   *take a minor road north, signed 'Hawridge Cholesbury',*
GR: 945069   *and this leads to Cholesbury after about 3 miles. The*
              directions start from the Full Moon, which is at the south
              end of the village and there are several parking spots by the
              common nearby.

THE FULL MOON PUB, CHOLESBURY

A book of adventurous pub walks would not be complete without an expedition to the highest point in the Chilterns, which lies at 876 ft above sea level in Wendover Woods. In truth, the point itself is not very exciting, being a commemorative cairn surrounded by trees a couple of hundred yards from the visitor centre and with no view. The monument on Coombe Hill (Walk 13) or Ivinghoe Beacon (Walk 18) are much more impressive. However, don't let that put you off as this expedition is well worth while for the superb walking, especially the woodland sections, and the excellent scenery – not to mention the cakes at the visitor centre.

This ridge at Cholesbury was once a busy route for driving cattle to market and numerous pubs in the area met the needs of the drovers. Now only a handful remain and one is the **Full Moon**, which dates back to the 17th century. It was the traditional meeting place for the Lord of the Manor of Hawridge to hold court, mainly concerned with the use of the commons, especially grazing rights and enclosures. For years, the traditional

Boxing Day Hunt met here, along with thousands of supporters. The pub has been waxing with the passing centuries: it was known as the Half Moon until 1812, the Moon until 1883 and the Full Moon ever since. It has a lovely garden, once a bowling green, and covered patio. For a lighter lunch there is a choice of sandwiches or jacket potatoes served with salad or something tasty from the starters menu such as mussels with garlic butter or nachos, as well as full meals. The beers include Adnams and Fuller's London Pride, plus guest ales that change twice weekly.

Telephone: *01494 758959.*

Alternatives: The Full Moon is the only pub on this route and the walk starts from there. If you wish to visit the pub halfway round you could start at the car park at Wendover Woods Visitor Centre (charge), following the directions from the end of point 7, though this has the disadvantage of a significant climb at the end of the walk. The Café in the Woods at the visitor centre serves sandwiches, snacks and excellent cakes and has tables inside and out. It is open every day from 9.30 am until 4.30 pm. There is also some roadside parking at point 6, The Hale, and this is my personal favourite for this walk, aiming for coffee (and cakes?) at the café and lunch at the Full Moon.

The Walk

Until 1935 Cholesbury did not have mains water, and drainage did not arrive until 1963. The road down to Chesham was frequently impassable in winter. Changes in agriculture and improved transport have resulted in it becoming a highly desirable place to live – with matching property prices.

❶ Continue through the village in the same direction, initially using a path parallel with the road on the left. Turn right along **Parrotts Lane** to the church on the right. Just through the church gates, turn left on a signed path along the Iron Age fort ramparts for about 120 yards, as far as a sort of ramp across the ditch on the right. Turn left and follow the path along the left-hand side of a wood then the left-hand side of two small fields back into woodland to meet a cross path. Turn left for 90 yards then, as the path swings right, bear left over a stile and follow the path to a lane. *(0.8 mile)*

The Iron Age 'fort', known as Cholesbury Camp, dates back to at least 100 BC but the site was occupied well before that. It was probably more of a trading centre than a military installation and a notice by the gate tells you all about it. The Norman church was built within the ramparts. By the 19th century it had fallen into disrepair but it was sympathetically restored.

2 Turn right for ¼ mile. Opposite **Harvest House** turn right on a signed cross path. Head across two fields to a lane. Cross the lane and keep ahead on a farm track. Just beyond the buildings go over a stile and continue in the same direction along the right-hand side of a field to a gate into a wood. Keep ahead at a cross path marked by waymarks on a post and walk through the wood to a track and lane. *(1.3 mile)*

3 Turn right along the lane for 20 yards then turn left on a signed path starting through a wooden kissing gate. Walk down the right-hand side of two small fields to a kissing gate into another wood. Follow the narrow path through the wood, then beside a wire fence to a surfaced drive and then ahead to a road. Turn left and shortly take the first lane on the right, signed 'The Hale', for 230 yards. *(0.5 mile)*

4 Turn right on a narrow signed path immediately before a house; this leads to a stile by a gate. Over the stile, bear round to the left and

you can see two gateways at the bottom of the field. Head for the one on the right then walk up the right-hand side of a field to a small gate some 20 yards to the left of a field gate. Cross a drive and press on along the waymarked path. Go over a stile and keep ahead on, at the time of writing, quite a faint path, crossing the **Ridgeway**. Maintain direction across a field when the path leaves a wood to find a cross path on the far side. *(0.6 mile)*

5 Turn left to a lane. Turn right. Immediately after the entrance to **Hale Farm Cottage** take a path to the right, parallel with the lane, to a track just after passing a pair of cottages. *(0.3 mile)*

6 Turn right on a signed path along the track. After about 90 yards, opposite a track on the right, bear left on a path. Follow this uphill as this joins a track. There is the alternative of a lovely parallel walkers' path, shown by footprint waymarks, first to the left and then to the right. If you stay on the track, bear round to the right as a track joins from the left. *(0.6 mile)*

This area has by no means always been as wooded as it is today. Just to the left at the top of the hill is another fort. The banks and ditch, which enclosed an area of about 17 acres, still exist to some extent, but are hard to see as they are now smothered in vegetation.

7 At the top, follow the main track round to the right and along the top of the ridge (the walkers' path emerges a couple of hundred yards along the ridge). Cross the access road to the car park and walk between the café and toilets to a wide green path. Turn right for 60 yards then left through **BBQ Area 3** to a cross path (note the carving on the right.) Turn right and the summit cairn is along a short path 100 yards on the left. *(0.7 mile)*

8 At the summit cairn turn left along a small path and follow this as it meanders through the trees then beside a fence. Continue as it turns away from the fence to the access road. Turn right along the road for just over 100 yards. *(0.5 mile)*

9 Just as the access road starts to go downhill, bear right on a waymarked path for about 300 yards to a waymarked cross

THE SUMMIT CAIRN AT POINT 8 OF THE ROUTE

path. Turn right to a stile then bear half left across a field, passing a trig point*, to a drive. Cross the drive to almost immediately reach a lane. Turn left for 20 yards then right on a signed path along a track. When the track ends at a gate, continue ahead on a path to the left of the gate down through trees to a tiny lane. *(1.1 mile)*

* The trig point marks the summit of Aston Hill but today the view is cut off by trees. The iconic Aston Martin cars took part of their name from this hill. Co-founder Lionel Martin used to race cars in the hill-climbing events that once took place here and was so inspired that he decided to add the name of the hill to his own for

the cars his firm made and so the famous brand was born.

⑩ Turn right for 120 yards then left on a signed path that shortly leads along the left-hand side of two fields to a hedged cross path, ignoring a crossing track at the end of the first field. *(0.5 mile)*

⑪ Turn right. Continue across a lane, now signed 'Leafy Lane Hastoe', and carry on along the track for about ¼ mile. *(0.4 mile)*

⑫ Turn left on a similar hedged track to a T-junction with a track. Turn right and follow the track uphill, ignoring paths to right and left, to the top of the ridge then continue along the track from a house called **Hastoe Grove** to a lane. *(0.7 mile)*

⑬ Turn left for a few yards then right and immediately right again on a track called **Browns Lane**. Remain on the track as it enters woodland. *(1.1 mile)*

These green lanes are byways left over when the modern road network was developed in the late 19th and early 20th centuries. They once criss-crossed the country but most became minor – or even major – roads.

⑭ Some 300 yards after the wood on the right thins, turn right on a

cross path signed 'Footpath 12' (the sign is less than obvious and is on the left) to a stile into a field. Walk along the left-hand side of the field to a lane. Turn left to a T-junction with a road. Cross the road and keep ahead across **Cholesbury Common**. After about 50 yards follow the path round to the right. The common is a maze of paths but essentially stick to this path (do not stray to the left) and head for the windmill behind the **Full Moon** when it comes into sight. *(0.7 mile)*

Cholesbury Windmill was first recorded in 1863 and continued to grind corn until the outbreak of the First World War, when it became a house. It has associations with artists and writers connected to the Bloomsbury Set who used to come and stay. Their doings at Cholesbury were depicted in pictures or formed the basis of several subsequent accounts in letters, memoirs and novels. The artist Mark Gertler painted a famous picture of the mill called 'Gilbert Cannan at his Mill', now on show at the Ashmolean in Oxford.

Date walk completed:

THE CHESS VALLEY
A sparkling Chiltern river

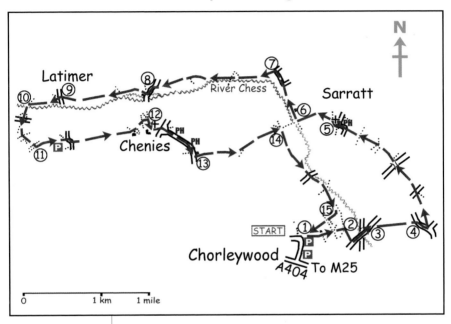

Distance:
9 miles

Map: OS Explorer 172 Chiltern Hills East

Starting Point:
Chorleywood
House Estate.
GR: 034970

How to get there: *The entrance to Chorleywood House Estate is on the A404, the Amersham–Rickmansworth road, about ½ mile west of junction 18 of the M25. Follow the entrance drive for about ¼ mile until it turns sharp left, where there is a parking area on the right. If this is full, there are several others; make your way through the park to this one, from where the directions start.*

99

THE RIVER CHESS

*T*he Chilterns are dry chalk hills with very few rivers. The most notable of those it does have is the Chess, which rises near Chesham and flows eleven miles through an attractive valley before joining the Colne. This walk explores the middle section. Part of the route lies beside the crystal clear water of the river and the rest uses paths high on the valley sides with some excellent views.

The **Cock Inn**, a Hall and Woodhouse pub, at the south end of Sarratt is opposite the 12th-century church and is more than 400 years old. Inside, we are warned of low ceilings ('Duck or Grouse', say the signs over the doorposts) and the main dining room is an ancient, pointy-roofed rural barn, with a forest of overhanging beams. Substantial portions of traditional English main courses such as lamb chops, steak and ale pie, and curry are the dishes of the day. For a lighter meal, they serve a choice of sandwiches, filled jacket potatoes or ploughman's lunch. There are lots of tables outside and the welcome could not be more cheerful or friendly.

Telephone: *01923 282908*.

Alternatives: The route also passes the Bedford Arms *(01923 283301)*, which has a lovely garden, and the Red Lion *(01923 282722)*, both in Chenies, if you want a break in the later part of the walk.

The Walk

At the end of the 19th century Lady Ela Russell, a relative of the Russells of Chenies, bought the Regency Chorleywood House and grounds. She modified and enlarged the house and developed the estate to be virtually self-sufficient, with its own farms and market garden, and generated her own electricity. In 1939, after her death, the house and grounds were purchased by Chorleywood Urban District Council as their council offices. Evacuees were housed in the mansion and prisoners of war in the grounds during the Second World War. When the building was no longer needed it was converted into flats but the park was kept as public open space.

❶ With your back to the drive, take the right-hand of two paths on the far side of the parking area, initially along a track. Keep ahead at **Dell**

Farm Cottage and follow the path down into the **Chess Valley**, ignoring all side paths, to a T-junction with a surfaced path. *(0.4 mile)*

❷ Turn right to a road. Turn left, crossing the M25 and, though this is not apparent, crossing the **River Chess** as well. *(0.3 mile)*

❸ Shortly before the road narrows turn right on a permissive path starting through a wooden kissing gate. Follow the narrow path up through the trees to a lane. *(0.3 mile)*

❹ Turn right for 200 yards then turn left on a public footpath, signed 'Sarratt Church 1'. Follow the path across a field to a stile onto a track and lane. Cross the lane and continue in the same direction along a track, signed 'Sarratt Church ¾'. Re-cross the M25 and keep ahead along the track, now signed 'Church End ½'. Maintain direction at a track on the left. Some 25 yards after this junction, the track itself turns left but again keep ahead, now on a grassy path. Go over a cross track and across two fields and up the right-hand side of a third to a lane. Turn right to **Sarratt church** and the **Cock Inn** a few yards to the right. *(1.3 mile)*

Sarratt was built on a ridge surrounded by forest, and dates from about AD 700, the story being that the original settlers were a family from Sweden. Until the 18th century Sarratt was a hamlet, clustered round the church. However, the village of Sarratt Green, about ¾ mile away, began to grow in the 17th century and eventually took the name of Sarratt, the original village becoming known as Church End. The church dates from the 12th century and has some 14th-century wall paintings. There is more information available within. You may recognise it as it was used as a location in the film **Four Weddings and a Funeral.**

5 Turn left in front of some almshouses then right, signed 'Chess Valley ½', to pass to the left of the church to a gate

and stile out of the churchyard. Over the stile, turn left to walk along the left-hand side of the field to a stile beside a gate. Over the stile, turn left, signed 'Chenies 1', with a superb view across the **Chess Valley**. Head down the left-hand side of the field then over a stile and continue downhill. *(0.4 mile)*

6 At the bottom, turn right on a wide path that soon becomes a drive to some cottages and leads to a tiny lane. Turn left along the lane as far as a right-hand bend. *(0.5 mile)*

7 At the bend, turn left along a surfaced track, signed 'Latimer 2'. When the track turns right towards a farm take a footpath slightly right, starting between metal barriers and along a boardwalk. **Do not cross the river.** Continue along this path

THE COCK INN, SARRATT

as it turns right away from the river and leads through woodland then on across water meadows to a lane. *(1 mile)*

The clean water of the Chess, bubbling out of the chalk at a constant 100°C, provides the ideal conditions for growing watercress. Water from the river and springs is diverted into a series of growing compartments or beds. The cress takes root in the shallow beds, taking minerals from the calcium-rich water. The Chess Valley used to be famous for its watercress but now only this one farm remains. You can buy it from the farm, if you are willing to carry quite a large bundle!

The path turns away from the river to skirt round Frogmore Meadow. Water meadows are often drained, to be ploughed up and replanted with modern strains of grass, with fertiliser and pesticides used on them. This makes them much less valuable for wildlife and so areas where this has never happened are important relics and Frogmore Meadow is one such.

8 Turn left for 120 yards then turn right through metal farm gates, passing to the right of a house, to walk beside a branch of the **Chess**. Ignore a path on the right and keep ahead on this path to a lane. *(0.7 mile)*

9 Cross the lane to find two signed paths starting through a wooden kissing gate. Take the path bearing half left to walk beside perhaps the most open and attractive stretch of the river, to a gate onto a surfaced drive. *(0.3 mile)*

The imposing house you can see up the hill is Latimer House. The Chess has been dammed here to create an artificial lake and the waterfall, on the right of the drive, is decorated with a statue of Neptune. The house is now a conference centre.

10 Turn left. When the drive shortly forks, go through a kissing gate ahead and slightly right across a field to a road. Cross the road and continue on the path for 20 yards. Now fork left to walk next to the fence on the left to a kissing gate into a wood. Immediately through the gate take the second path to the left. When the path forks after 20 yards, take the left, less steep fork and climb through the wood to a T-junction with a cross path just inside the wood. *(0.4 mile)*

11 Turn left and follow the path to a lane. Turn right along the lane for about 50 yards then turn left on a signed bridleway along a track opposite a parking area, initially along the top edge of a wood. Continue along the track when it leaves the wood. When the track bears slightly right as you approach a house, keep ahead through a wooden kissing gate on a path through woodland and follow the path as it bears left after 50 yards. *(1 mile)*

⓬ At the end of the wood turn right along a cross path up into **Chenies** to emerge by the gates of **Chenies Manor**. Turn left down the drive to the village green. Cross the green and go ahead out of the village on a road signed 'Chorleywood 1¾ Rickmansworth 4', passing the **Bedford Arms** then the **Red Lion**. *(0.5 mile)*

Chenies (pronounced Chainies) used to be called Isenhampstead. In the Middle Ages the manor was owned by the Cheyne family and eventually the original name was dropped. The manor passed to the Russell family in 1526. The Russells became the Earls and Dukes of Bedford in 1550. They rebuilt the manor house and created the family mausoleum in the adjacent church, said to be the best collection of funeral monuments in any parish church in England. More information about the church is given in the very comprehensive booklet available within. Death duties forced the Russells to sell Chenies after the death of the twelfth Duke in 1954, though they had long since moved

to Woburn Abbey. Henry VIII visited Chenies Manor twice and Elizabeth I paid three visits while it was still the main Russell residence. The manor is open to the public on Wednesday and Thursday between April and October and all Bank Holiday Mondays, from 2 pm to 5 pm. Telephone: 01494 762888.

⓭ Immediately after a red brick house with numerous chimneys turn left through a small wooden gate on the **Chiltern Way**. Follow the waymarked path gently downhill through woods, across a field, and through more woods to a gate at the bottom of the woods. *(0.7 mile)*

⓮ Through the gate, turn right on a cross path signed 'Sarratt Mill ¼'. Cross a lane and continue ahead, signed 'Solesbridge Lane ¾'. Follow the main path ahead for a bare ½ mile. *(0.8 mile)*

⓯ Turn right, signed 'Chorleywood House Estate ¾'. Ignore all side turns and follow the path up the valley side, back to the parking area where this walk started. *(0.4 mile)*

Date walk completed:

PITSTONE HILL AND THE GRAND UNION CANAL
The way through the hills

THE GRAND UNION CANAL

Distance: 8½ miles	**Map:** OS Explorer 181 Chiltern Hills North
Starting Point: Pitstone Hill car park. GR: 955149	**How to get there:** *From the B488, the Ivinghoe–Tring road, ½ mile south of its junction with the B489, take a minor road to a car park on the right after ½ mile.*

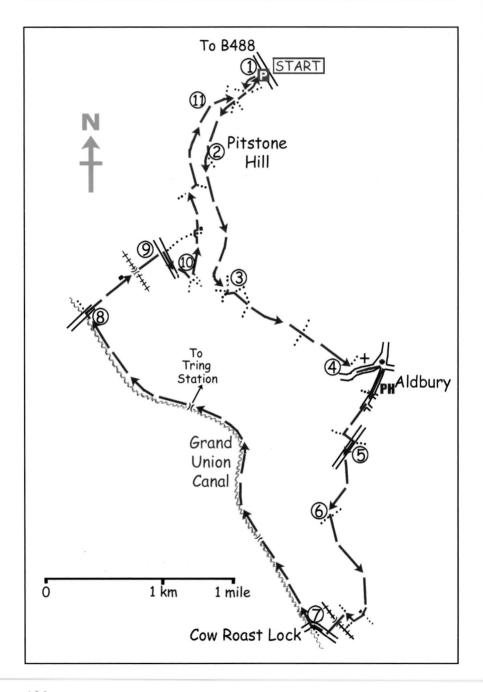

*T*his is an immensely varied walk that starts with the wide-open downland and extensive views of Pitstone Hill before traversing the beautiful woods of Aldbury Nowers to the picture-postcard village of Aldbury and its 18th-century pub. The route then winds its way by field paths into Tring Gap and the summit of the Grand Union Canal for a two-mile walk beside one of its prettiest stretches, made more interesting by the narrowboats that chug their way through the Chilterns.

The **Valiant Trooper** at Aldbury is housed in two 17th-century cottages that have been an alehouse for several centuries – at least since 1752 when it was mentioned in a will. It became known as the Trooper in 1803 after the Duke of Wellington, featured on the pub sign, is said to have met there with his troops to discuss tactics for the Napoleonic War. There are two cosy bars with open fires in the winter and plenty of tables in the garden at the back, as well as a separate restaurant. They serve a good selection of real ales including Trooper from Tring Brewery and several guest beers. The lunchtime menu features a choice of tasty sandwiches, as well as ploughman's and pub favourites.

Telephone: *01442 851203.*

Alternatives: Aldbury also has the Greyhound *(01442 851228),* in the centre of the village.

If you wish to start by the canal there is parking at Tring station, near the canal (between points 7 and 8), and a few roadside spaces near Cow Roast Lock (end of point 6). Parking in Aldbury is very limited and the village car park is outside the village, not directly on the route.

The Walk

Carry on over the brow of the hill and follow the wide grassy path up over **Pitstone Hill**. *(0.6 mile)*

❶ Go through a gate at the rear of the car park, more or less opposite the entrance to the car park, and follow the path to the top of the hill.

Like many of the promontories of the Chiltern escarpment, Pitstone Hill is crowned with the remains of prehistoric earthworks. They are much more apparent here because of the open landscape, maintained by grazing.

2 Do not continue on the grassy path round to the left but opt for the waymarked **Ridgeway**, slightly down and round the hill and then through **Aldbury Nowers**. Continue on the Ridgeway, down steps, as a path joins from the left. *(0.8 mile)*

THE VALIANT TROOPER PUB

Aldbury Nowers is a nature reserve because of the many species of butterflies to be found on these warm, south-west facing slopes. The insects are attracted by the variety of flowers that produce nectar on which the butterflies feed. The open grassland is not crossed on this walk but is easily accessible from the path.

3 At the bottom of the steps leave the **Ridgeway** and turn left on a signed path for 40 yards, then turn right on a path shown by waymark arrows on a post. Keep ahead over a cross path immediately after leaving the wood and continue across a golf course on the path marked by a series of posts. Go over a stile at the end of the golf course onto a cross path and continue in the same direction on a path a few yards to the right, signed 'Aldbury 0.4 miles'. Follow this to a road. *(0.8 mile)*

As you walk across the golf course, ahead and slightly left, on top of

the hill, the Bridgewater Monument can be seen. This is visited on Walk 18.*

4 Turn left into **Aldbury**. Turn right along **Trooper Road**. Continue ahead at the **Valiant Trooper**. At the end of the road continue in the same direction on a signed path, initially between hedges. After 40 yards go through a metal kissing gate on the left and keep ahead along the right-hand side of a field. At the end of the field go through a gate and turn left to a lane. *(0.7 mile)*

Aldbury hugs the base of the escarpment. It must be one of the most visited and photographed villages in the Chilterns. It has all the necessary ingredients: a wealth of old and charming buildings in a great variety of styles, a large pond well supplied with ducks and a village green

complete with stocks and
whipping post. These reminders of
a more brutal past were once
found on every village green and
used to punish crimes such as
playing games on Sunday, as well
as more serious offences.

5 Turn right along the lane for
200 yards. Turn left on a path signed
'Cow Roast 1¼' that leads half right
across three small fields. At the far
side of the third field turn right to
walk along the edge of a wood on
the left. *(0.4 mile)*

6 At the end of the wood turn left
up to a kissing gate into a field. Bear
half right down the field to find a
gate into a strip of woodland and
then a field. Turn left along the left-
hand side of the field to a stile. Over
the stile, bear diagonally right across
a field to the left of farm buildings
seen ahead, to a stile. Over the
stile, go ahead for a few yards then
turn left along the farm track for
15 yards. Turn right along a track. At
the end of the first field on the right,
turn right on a signed bridleway for
90 yards then turn left across a field
and the railway to a lane. Turn right
to the **Grand Union Canal** at **Cow
Roast Lock**. *(1 mile)*

*This is Tring Gap, which has been
an important route through the
Chilterns since Roman times as we
can see from the road, canal and
railway all close together. The*

*main road at the end of this lane,
now the A41, was a major Roman
road called Akeman Street. The
railway is the main London to
Birmingham line from Euston.
It opened as far as Tring station
in October 1837, then to
Birmingham the following year.
The canal was built by the Grand
Junction Canal Company, formed
in 1793, and significantly
shortened the route to London
from Birmingham by avoiding the
winding Oxford Canal and the
River Thames. Constructing the
canal over the Chilterns was a
major feat of engineering. Cow
Roast Lock is the summit of the
canal. Its name does not, as might
be imagined, refer to some
gigantic barbecue but is a
corruption of the term Cow Rest.
This was a favourite resting place
for drovers as they took cattle
through the Chilterns to the
London markets.*

7 Immediately before the bridge
over the canal, turn right to walk
with the canal on the left for a good
2 miles to the third bridge over the
canal. *(2.1 miles)*

*The canal is in a cutting for part
of the way. This was excavated
to reduce the number of locks
needed for two reasons: to make
passage easier and also because
water has always been a problem
for this canal in the dry Chilterns.*

Every time the lock gates are opened some water is lost and this has to be replenished. Several reservoirs had to be constructed to supply this water and these are still in use today.

8 Just before the bridge the towpath leaves the canal and climbs to a surfaced drive. Turn right along the drive, signed 'Aldbury Nowers 1'. Continue past a farm and over the railway to a road. *(0.5 mile)*

9 Turn right for 160 yards then left on a bridleway, signed 'Aldbury 1¼', to a cross track. *(0.3 mile)*

10 Turn left and follow the track gently uphill, crossing a drive, to a barn. Go through a small gate to the left on a signed path and follow this to a second small gate and a cross path. Turn right for 75 yards to yet another small gate. Through this gate turn left. The path is initially by a fence on the left, diverges from it and then comes back to the fence as it contours round the hill. *(1 mile)*

One feature of the view you cannot fail to notice is the quarry at the foot of the hill. This was dug for chalk, used at the cement works at Pitstone village that closed in the 1990s. The quarry is now closed, though some chalk is removed from the site for agricultural use. The future of the quarry has been the subject of

long and difficult negotiations and is still unresolved at the time of writing. A big hole in the ground is a valuable asset and the owners want to use it as a landfill site. Despite considerable opposition, Bucks County Council agreed that it could be used for inert material provided it was landscaped afterwards. However, the details have yet to be resolved. In particular, the rocks beneath are an important aquifer from which water is extracted and this needs to be protected against possible pollution from the material dumped. Much less obvious in the view is Pitstone Windmill, which is thought to be oldest windmill in England. It dates from at least the 17th century and possibly earlier. It ceased operation in 1902 when it was damaged in a storm and was restored in the 1960s. It is open to the public on summer Sundays (01442 851227).

11 Shortly after a gate on the left follow the path to the right uphill to the broad cross path used near the start of the walk. Turn left and skirt round to the right of the hill back to the start. *(0.4 mile)*

Date walk completed:

IVINGHOE BEACON
Views, views and more views

THE VIEW FROM ALDBURY COMMON

Distance:	Map: OS Explorer 181 Chiltern Hills North
9½ miles	

Starting Point: Clipper Down car park. GR: 964155

How to get there: *From the B4506, the Berkhamsted–Dagnall road, about 5 miles north of Berkhamsted at Ringshall, take Beacon Road for about 1½ miles to an informal parking area on the left just after a cattle grid.*

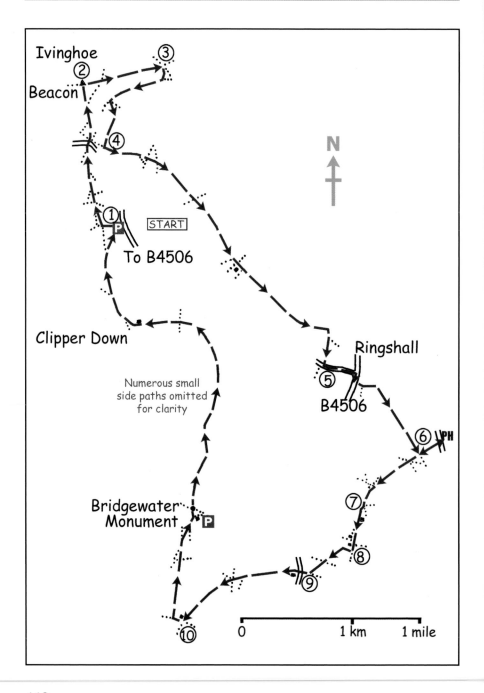

Ivinghoe
② ③
Beacon
④

N

① P
START
To B4506

Clipper Down

Numerous small
side paths omitted
for clarity

Ringshall
⑤
B4506

⑥ PH

⑦

Bridgewater
Monument P
⑧

⑨

⑩

0   1 km   1 mile

*T*he panoramic view from the parking place where this walk starts gives a foretaste of what is to come on this outstanding route. This is the walk in the Chilterns I would recommend to someone who only had time for one (or would I, when so many other treats spring to mind!). It has so much of what makes the Chilterns special – magnificent views that stretch for miles, beautiful woods and an abundance of human and natural history, all made accessible by a network of well-maintained paths. Enjoy!

The **Bridgewater Arms** in Little Gaddesden has been a pub since the 18th century and still welcomes visitors, with its cosy log fire in winter and pleasant garden in summer. According to the menu, it once also housed the village school and the children had to climb through a window, as they could not go through the door of licensed premises. There is now a restaurant in the old school room and the flagged public bar is decorated with photos of a well-known local character, Old Shep. The food is delicious and includes something for every appetite, from sandwiches and wraps, light meals such as smoked salmon and crème fraîche tart through to full meals, all rounded off with tempting puds. I particularly enjoyed the deli board to share (and no, I didn't eat it all myself!). Greene King IPA and Abbot Ale are always available and the third pump is a guest ale that rotates with every barrel.

Telephone: *01442 842408.*

Alternatives: An equally feasible plan, though the pub is then quite late in the walk, is to start at the Bridgewater Monument partway through point 10, accessed from the B4506, where there is a large car park. There are no other pubs on this route but there is an excellent National Trust tearoom at the monument.

 *The Walk*

1 Take a path at the rear of the car park, starting between wooden posts and about 20 yards to the right of the track to **Clipper Down Cottage**. This crosses the ridge to shortly meet a cross path with fantastic views in the other direction. Turn right and follow this path to the top of **Ivinghoe Beacon**, which soon comes into view. *(0.9 mile)*

*The views from this point are
panoramic. The range of hills seen
to the north-east are the
Dunstable Downs and the lower,
tree-covered ridge to the left of
them is Totternhoe Knolls, both
explored on Walk 19. Many chalk
hills have a horse carved into them
but in the Chilterns we have a lion,
marking the presence of
Whipsnade Zoo.*

2 At the trig point, turn right along
the ridge as far as a fence across the
path. *(0.5 mile)*

3 Turn right beside the fence then
fork right to a path along the bottom
of the hill. Walk with the fence on
your left. When the fence ends do
not continue on the obvious path
ahead but fork half left (not full left
by the fence to a gate) on a path that
cuts across to soon walk by the fence
again to a field gate. *(0.7 mile)*

4 Go through the field gate and
turn left. As you pass a kissing gate
on the left ignore a right fork uphill
and cross paths to reach a kissing
gate by a field gate into woodland.
Press on along the main waymarked
path, eventually climbing very
steeply, assisted by steps. At the top
continue towards farm buildings
along the right-hand side of a small
field and pass to the left of all the
buildings. Keep ahead on the
waymarked path across three fields
then beside a wood. Follow the path,

now enclosed between a fence and
hedge, round a sharp right-hand
bend, in fact skirting **Ringshall
reservoir**, and carry on along the
track to a road. *(1.8 miles)*

5 Turn left. At a T-junction with
the B4506 turn right for 30 yards
then left on a path signed 'Little
Gaddesden ⅔'. Ignore a path on the
right after 80 yards then later
follow the path round a right-hand
bend. Keep ahead as the path
becomes a surfaced drive to a
signed cross path at the end of a
short stretch with a wooden fence
on the left. *(0.8 mile)*

*This valley is called Witchcraft
Bottom and is said to be where
the last witch in Buckinghamshire
was tried and executed. This
connection was given added
impetus when Gerald Massey, an
impoverished poet and journalist,
came to live here in the 1860s. His
first wife, Rosina, was a noted
clairvoyant and given to bouts of
depression and drunkenness,
possibly brought on by the deaths
of two of her children. Her
behaviour aroused deep
superstitions in the villagers, who
came to believe her to be a witch.
For example, one evening a small
boy was passing the cottage and
claimed he saw Rosina with her
hands outstretched, apparently
moving some cups and saucers on
a table without human contact.*

THE BRIDGEWATER ARMS, LITTLE GADDESDEN

Rosina was probably using an ouija board but the idea that she must be a witch began to spread. Other incidents added to the story, such as when she was said to have had a row with a local farmer and cast a spell on his cattle so they gave no milk, always a favourite accusation against suspected witches. She died in 1866 at the age of 34 and is buried in Little Gaddesden.

6 Turn left up some steps to reach the **Bridgewater Arms** after a couple of hundred yards, then return to this point. To continue the route turn right (straight on if coming from the pub) and follow the path as it crosses part of a golf course then between a fence and hedge and across a drive to arrive at a junction of drives. Keep ahead along a drive, ignoring a path to the right after 40 yards. *(0.6 mile)*

As you walk across this part of the Ashridge Estate you get some idea of what might have happened to all of it without the intervention of the National Trust. The golf course is attractive enough in its way but there are also several large houses in their own lavish plots. The Egerton family owned the estate until 1921 when the will of the final private owner decreed it was to be sold. Up until then people in the area had enjoyed the freedom of this beautiful estate but that soon changed as the trustees set about disposing of it piecemeal. Fortunately, some influential people were appalled. A public appeal brought an outstanding response, especially locally, and enabled the National Trust to buy 1,700 acres immediately and other parcels of land since.

7 Just before the clubhouse car park bear right on a signed path and follow this from waymark to waymark across more of the golf course. Keep to the left of a track leading to buildings and then the buildings themselves. *(0.3 mile)*

8 Immediately after **Old Park Lodge** turn right on a waymarked path for 125 yards. At a waymark post turn left across a fairway and through a narrow belt of trees to a wide grassy path with a view of **Ashridge House** to the left and the **Bridgewater Monument**, passed

later in the walk, to the right. Cross this and carry on along the path. This is not obvious at the time of writing, though marked with occasional waymarks, but maintain direction to find a surfaced drive. *(0.3 mile)*

Ashridge House is the latest building on this site. An abbey was established here in 1283 and Richard, Earl of Cornwall, Henry III's brother, donated a golden box containing what was said to be a phial of Christ's blood that he had brought back from the Crusades. For 250 years the abbey attracted many pilgrims and became wealthy. One such visitor was King Edward I who held Parliament here in 1290 while he spent Christmas in nearby Pitstone. When Henry VIII suppressed the monastery in 1539 the relic was shown to be a fake of, it is said, coloured honey. It became a home for his children and the future Elizabeth I was staying here in 1554 when she was arrested on suspicion of being involved in a plot to remove Mary from the throne. The present building dates from the early 19th century and is now a well-known management college. It is not owned by the National Trust but is open to the public occasionally.

9 Turn right to a road. Cross the road and keep ahead on a signed path, past **Thunderdell Cottages**, for just over ¼ mile to a wide crossing path followed immediately by a split in the path. Take the left option to continue in the same direction to a wooden gate by a house. *(0.8 mile)*

⑩ Immediately after the house, turn right. After 100 yards bear right, ignoring a path going straight on. This is a bridleway. There is a more or less parallel walkers' path to the right but the views are not as good and the bridleway is not usually churned up so it is better to stick to this. Follow this, ignoring all side turns, to the **Bridgewater Monument**. Do not follow the path round to the right to the visitor centre and tearoom but cut across a grassy area, passing the monument, and take a path ahead, signed 'Mobility Vehicles Trail'. Stay on this wonderful path and it eventually leads back to the car park where this walk started*. *(2.7 miles)*

This 108 ft high pillar was erected to commemorate the life and works of Francis Egerton, 3rd Duke of Bridgewater. He inherited the title aged 11 in 1748 when his brother died. A sickly child, he was thought to be of such limited intellectual capacity that serious consideration was given to breaking the entail to prevent him inheriting. He became engaged to a great society beauty but when the engagement ended he retired to the country, swearing he would never again speak to a woman; he kept his word as far as is known and devoted himself to building canals, working with an illiterate but inspired engineer called James Brindley. One supplied the cash and the other the know-how to build the first entirely artificial canal in Britain, to carry coal from the Duke's mines at Worsley into Manchester. It cut the price of coal in the city by half and inspired a transport revolution. He accumulated great wealth through his canal and coal interests and started to redevelop Ashridge. He died in 1803 before his plans came to fruition, leaving his heirs with a pile of rubble. The monument is often open in the summer and if you have the energy for the 172 steps, you will be rewarded with magnificent views (as if there aren't enough on this walk!).

(*If you started this walk at the **Bridgewater Monument**, after 2½ miles take a path on the left immediately after a cattle grid: this is the path to **Ivinghoe Beacon** followed in point 1.)

Date walk completed:

DUNSTABLE DOWNS
Kites and gliders

LOOKING TOWARDS DUNSTABLE DOWNS

Distance:
9½ miles

You will need a veritable library for this one as it is at the corner of four maps – OS Explorer 181 and 182 plus 192 and 193

Starting Point:
Bison Hill
car park.
GR: 999184

How to get there: *From the B489, the Dunstable–Ivinghoe road, about 3 miles south of Dunstable, take the B4506, signed 'Dagnall'. After ¼ mile fork left on the B4540, signed 'Whipsnade', to a car park on the left.*

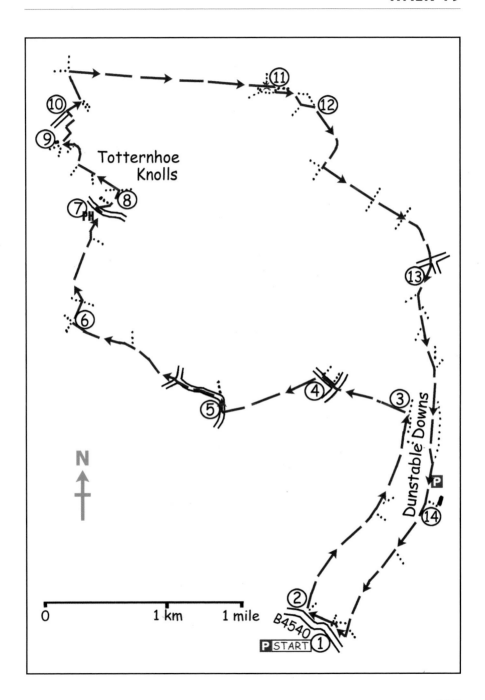

Totternhoe
Knolls

Dunstable Downs

N

0   1 km   1 mile

B4540

P START

*T*his is perhaps the most varied walk in this book and has many features of interest. Be sure to keep your eyes open to see the many objects both natural and man-made that soar above the Downs, taking advantage of the thermals these hills generate. The route starts on the shoulder of the Downs near Whipsnade Zoo at the aptly-named Bison Hill car park and first skirts the base of the hills, a home for many butterflies and wildflowers. It then crosses the Vale to an outlying hill, Totternhoe Knolls, before returning to the top of the Downs for an exhilarating ridge walk back to the start.

The **Cross Keys** in Totternhoe is a charming 14th-century pub complete with thatch, tiled floors and inglenook fireplaces – and a warm welcome. It has a huge garden with lovely views and some of the damson trees for which this area was once famous. They serve good pub grub from sandwiches and filled jacket potatoes through ploughman's lunches and burgers to full meals, supplemented by daily specials. The four cask ales include Greene King IPA, Abbot and Broadside and a guest beer such as Springhead Roaring Meg and Marston's Old Empire.

Telephone: *01525 220434.*

Alternatives: There is no other pub on the route but the Gateway Centre at Dunstable Downs (point 14) has an excellent café run by the National Trust *(01582 500920)*.

The Walk

❶ With your back to the entrance to the car park, take a path leading from the left rear corner. After some 50 yards turn left along a cross path, soon going steeply downhill with a guard fence on the left. *(0.2 mile)*

❷ At the bottom of the hill turn

right along a broad, hedged bridleway that leads along the base of the slope. There is a parallel walkers' path for much of the way and the lower bridleway turns right to join this soon after a gate. Some 100 yards further on the path forks: be careful to bear left here as the right fork climbs to the visitor centre, shortening the route by many miles. When the path forks again, take the left option to reach a gate on the left at the end of the gliding field. *(1.1 mile)*

You cannot help but notice the activities of the London Gliding Club to the left of the path. It was formed in 1930 and used Ivinghoe Beacon as a launch site for its gliders. The spectacle attracted so much attention that they were evicted for spoiling the peace of the countryside and moved to a permanent home here.

❸ Turn left through the gate on a signed bridleway. Cross a major road and continue in the same direction along **Wellhead Road** for 120 yards to a signed bridleway on the left opposite a footpath on the right. *(0.5 mile)*

❹ Turn left to eventually reach a lane. *(0.6 mile)*

❺ Turn right along the lane. At a T-junction with a road continue in the same direction on a signed bridleway. Ignore a signed bridleway on the right. *(0.9 mile)*

❻ Just before a track on the left, turn right on a waymarked path along the left-hand side of a field heading for **Totternhoe**, backed by the **Knolls**. At the end of the field go over a stile and cross path and bear slightly left to the corner of a hedge then keep ahead with the hedge on the right. At the end of this field

press on ahead, soon rising to the road through Totternhoe. Turn left to the **Cross Keys**. *(0.7 mile)*

Totternhoe is a long thin village strung out along the base of the Knolls. There has been a village here since time immemorial and a fine Roman villa has been excavated locally. The Anglo-Saxons contributed the name, which appears in the Domesday Book as Totenehou, meaning 'the look out house on the spur', no doubt referring to forts on the hills above.

❼ Almost opposite the pub, turn right on a signed path and follow this uphill to a T-junction with a cross path. *(0.2 mile)*

❽ Turn left. Follow the main path along the top of the **Knolls** and then downhill, ignoring paths to the left. *(0.5 mile)*

The path passes the site of both Totternhoe Castle and some of the numerous quarries to be found in this area. The castle was a Norman motte and bailey and remarkably little is known about exactly when or by whom it was built. None of the buildings remain but the mound or motte and baileys or outer walls can still be made out on the ground. It was certainly built in a commanding position and a recent geophysical survey has suggested that it was constructed on the site of earlier structures, possibly dating back to Roman times or even earlier. Totternhoe stone is a very pure form of chalk that is particularly good for stone carving and has been used for centuries, including the Roman villa referred to earlier and in many important buildings, among them Westminster Abbey and Windsor Castle. It is used for indoor construction because it does not have good weather resistance outside as it holds a lot of water. The disused quarries are now managed as nature reserves and support a rich variety of flowers and insects that live on them.

9 Just before the first building on the right take a waymarked path on the right, almost back on yourself, and follow the fenced path to emerge at the end of a road. *(0.2 mile)*

10 Turn right. At a cross track just before the track turns right, turn left to a surfaced cross path. Turn right along this disused railway line. *(1.3 mile)*

The railway here was built in 1848 to link Dunstable to the main line at Leighton Buzzard. It closed in 1967 and is now managed as a nature reserve.

11 Some 50 yards after crossing a bridge over a track turn right then immediately left on an initially parallel track. After about 200 yards bear right on a waymarked path. Keep to the right-hand side of the field but do not go through a gap on the right into a large, roughly circular area*. Instead, keep ahead with a hedge and bank on the right to shortly reach a gap in the hedge on the left and a gravelled track. *(0.3 mile)*

*This is Maiden Bower, the remains of an Iron Age hill fort on private property. There is not a lot to see – a roughly circular hedged area – for somewhere that has such a long history dating back perhaps 5,000 years. Excavations have shown there was a Neolithic burial here and, much later, an Iron Age hill fort and then possibly a Roman temple.

12 Turn right. Stay on this track as it bends right and left to arrive at a main road at a roundabout. *(1.1 mile)*

13 Cross the road and bear slightly right uphill, signed 'Icknield Way Trail'. Ignore paths forking right and left and keep ahead to the top of the hill, passing intriguing humps. At the top bear right and follow a surfaced path. When this forks take either branch as they rejoin further on (the right has better views) and press on towards the visitor centre seen ahead. *(1.2 mile)*

The intriguing humps are burial mounds dating to the later Neolithic and early Bronze Ages. All but three have been excavated, the most recent dig being in the 1920s when it was found that nearly 100 bodies had been dumped in mass graves on top of the prehistoric remains. Most were young men and some had their hands tied behind their backs. Objects found with them suggest they were Saxon so perhaps they were involved in a local battle.

The prominent position of the Downs means they have been used in local signalling systems when England has been under threat. One of the chain of Armada beacons was built here in the 16th century when Spain threatened. A couple of centuries later the danger came from France and Napoleon when there was real fear of invasion. One of a chain of semaphore signalling stations was established on the Downs. They used a system of six shutters whose positions made up a code and its main purpose was to transmit intelligence and orders between London and Great Yarmouth.

⑭ The surfaced path turns left to the visitor centre at a curious metal structure**. At this point bear slightly right to continue in the same direction on a signed path along the top of the slope. Ignore a path on the left to **Whipsnade village** and keep on in the same direction, signed 'Bison Hill car park ½ mile, Ivinghoe Beacon 7¼ miles' to eventually arrive at some steps on the right that lead down to the car park where this walk started. *(0.8 mile)*

**The Bedfordshire County Council/National Trust visitor facility uses a whole range of green devices to reduce its environmental impact – and sells good cakes too. As well as wood-chip burners, heat reflecting windows and air-flushed lavatories, the metal structure is a wind-catcher that cools the building in summer and warms it in winter.

Date walk completed:

SUNDON HILLS AND SHARPENHOE CLAPPERS

The undiscovered Chilterns

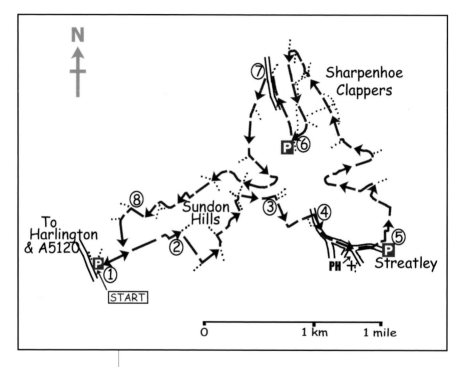

Distance:
7 miles

Map: OS Explorer 193 Luton & Stevenage

Starting Point:
Sundon Hills
car park.
GR: 047285

How to get there: *From the A5120, the Dunstable–Ampthill road, ½ mile north-east of junction 12 on the M1 at a roundabout, take a minor road east, signed 'Harlington'. At a crossroads in Harlington turn right, signed 'Sundon', for 1½ miles to a car park on the left.*

SHARPENHOE CLAPPERS

*N*o doubt the residents of Luton and surrounding area will not be impressed by my subtitle as they have this attractive area on their doorstep. However, it is often said that the Chilterns lie between Goring and Ivinghoe Beacon but that is a misconception as both the hills themselves and the AONB extend further north-east and deserve to be better appreciated by a wider public. This walk explores the part known as the **Sundon Hills** and **Sharpenhoe Clappers**, which are towards the north-eastern end of the scarp slope visited by several other walks in this book. No other route has so much walking right on the edge with superb views both out across the plain and into the steep-sided valleys that nibble into the slope. Much of the area is managed for wildlife and is rich in wildflowers, birds and butterflies. This is a great area for bluebells in spring and blackberries in autumn with a profusion of large, sweet berries; slip a bag into your pack if you are doing this walk in September. The route may look a bit odd on the map but is great on the ground – so have the adventure of crossing the M1 and enjoy the undiscovered Chilterns.

The **Chequers** in Streatley is an attractive village pub that dates from Georgian times. It has a large patio in front shaded by an oak tree. The chunky sandwiches live up to their name and the full meals include steak and ale pie as one of the favourites on the menu. A Greene King house, they stock five real ales including Old Speckled Hen and a guest beer.

Telephone: 01582 882072.

Alternatives: There is no other source of refreshment on this route. If you wish to visit the pub later in the walk there is an alternative public car park at Sharpenhoe Clappers at point 6.

The Walk

❶ With your back to the entrance, go through a metal kissing gate at the far end of the car park (not the gates on the left) and keep ahead along the top of the slope with a fence on the right for ½ mile. *(0.5 mile)*

❷ Turn right through a metal kissing gate and walk along the left-hand side of a field to find a cross path at the far end. Turn left to walk along the right-hand side of a field with a wood on the right. At the end of the wood bear left along a track, soon walking with another wood on the right. When this ends turn right on a waymarked path round the wood. Follow this round a sharp left-hand bend. After a further 90 yards turn right into the wood. Turn left. After 30 yards do not go down some steps ahead but turn right to stay on top of the slope for about 300 yards. *(0.9 mile)*

❸ Turn right on a waymarked path. Ignore a track on the left after 20 yards and keep ahead on a path between a fence and a hedge. When the fence ends follow the path round to the left. At the end of the field keep ahead to a road. *(0.4 mile)*

❹ Turn right. At a junction turn left, signed 'Barton 2'. At the **Chequers** turn left along **Church Road**, using the footway on the left. Stay on the footway, to the left of a parking area,

THE CHEQUERS IN STREATLEY

to find a path signed 'Icknield Way', just before the main road, the A6. *(0.5 mile)*

The name Streatley means the clearing by the street and the village once lay on an important road that became the A6, now to the east of the village. It was not a major Roman road but was established as a significant route by medieval times. The church, behind the pub, has a long list of vicars. James Hadrow served the parish for 59 years, from 1781 until 1840. He married Sarah Wye in 1788. The Wye family did not approve of the liaison and sent her off to her uncle in Yorkshire. One night when the family were going out to a ball she stayed at home, pleading ill health, and eloped with James instead. They were married for 52 years and had eight children so it was obviously a success.

5 Turn left along this path. As you approach a wood follow the permissive path round to the left then keep on the wide grassy path as it twists and turns along the top of the very steep slope with dramatic views down into the very steep small valleys, known as holes. After passing through a gate into National Trust land turn right to continue along the top of the slope. Immediately after entering woodland the path becomes less obvious.

Ignore the clear path on the left and a smaller one bearing slightly right. Instead, bear slightly left up over the roots of two beech trees to join a path coming in from the left and continue round the end of the hill and back along the other side. When the path forks bear left, not right down some steps, and ignore all side paths. Press on when it becomes a surfaced track to finally arrive at a car park. *(2.5 miles)*

Sharpenhoe Clappers is a classic chalk escarpment standing out like the prow of an ocean liner from the surrounding plain. Among the beeches you can make out the earthwork remains of two terraces on the northern slope and two banks that run across the spur to the south. They were believed to be an Iron Age fort but an archaeological dig carried out in 1979 showed that the bank dated to medieval times and had been built as a rabbit warren. The existence of warrens in the Sharpenhoe area is suggested by the 'Clappers' name, which is from an old French word for rabbit warren. Rabbits are not native to Britain: they originated in the Iberian peninsula and were brought to England by the Normans for food and fur. The medieval rabbit was regarded as a poor and helpless, albeit tasty and nutritious, creature that needed to be carefully nursed from cradle

to stew-pot. *Consequently,
artificial warrens had to be made.
These were mounds of soft earth,
often with pre-formed burrows.
The warrens were usually
enclosed to keep predators, such
as foxes at bay and were the
responsibility of a special official
called a warrener. Thus protected
the rabbits thrived until, by the
17th or 18th century, they had
adapted to the harsh English
conditions, jumped the bounds of
their warrens and discovered the
delights of life on the other side
of the fence – and went on to
become a significant pest. The dig
also found that the rabbit warren
was overlying earlier features,
including a ditch and a palisade
trench that would once have held
timber posts and date to the Iron
Age. Roman artefacts have also
been found at the site.*

6 Immediately after going through
the gate into the car park turn right
downhill and continue along the
bottom of the valley to a gap in
the hedge on the left immediately
before a metal kissing gate.
(0.4 mile)

7 Turn left through the gap and
cross a road to take a signed path
opposite. Follow this path to the
base of the steep slope then
continue round to the right to
walk along the base of the slope,
ignoring all paths to left and right.
Immediately after passing through
a gate be sure to take the right,
lower, fork and press on until the
path passes an open area on the
left and starts to climb a short,
steep incline. *(1.6 mile)*

8 About three-quarters of the
way up the slope, as the gradient
becomes a bit less steep, bear
half left on a faint path uphill
to a disused chalk pit and a
bench overlooking it. Turn left
to a gate. Through the gate, head
across a field to find the path
used on the outward leg on the
far side and turn right, back to
the start. *(0.3 mile)*

*The chalk pit has long been
softened with vegetation. Note
how the rabbits have made their
burrows in the sides, with the
warmer south side being the
overwhelmingly favoured address.*

 Date walk completed: